WALTZ WITH ME

RENARD PRESS — PLAYSCRIPT VII

WALTZ WITH ME

DIANE SAMUELS

RENARD PRESS

RENARD PRESS LTD

124 City Road
London EC1V 2NX
United Kingdom
info@renardpress.com
020 8050 2928

www.renardpress.com

Waltz With Me first published by Renard Press Ltd in 2023

Text © Diane Samuels, 2023
Foreword © Ghislaine Kenyon, 2023
Quote by Sister Anne Murphy on p. 154 used with permission from the
Society of the Holy Child Jesus

Inside images © the Society of the Holy Child Jesus European Province Archives
Cover image © Smallfish Designs
Design by Will Dady

Printed in the United Kingdom by Severn

ISBN: 978-1-80447-042-8

9 8 7 6 5 4 3 2 1

Renard Press is proud to be a climate positive publisher, removing more carbon
from the air than we emit and planting a small forest. For more information see
renardpress.com/eco.

CONTENTS

FOREWORD

Nuns of the order known as the Society of the Holy Child Jesus (SHCJ) were my teachers throughout my schooldays: I was a day girl at Cavendish Square School in London and then a boarder at St Leonards-Mayfield in rural Sussex. And so perhaps it was not so surprising that when I finally left this convent education behind for the freeing new world of Oxford University I buried it. Not as a conscious act, but it must have seemed to me a given that the person at the centre of this next bit of life would share little with the one from the confined and confining universe of Mayfield. I graduated, decided I wanted to become a primary-school teacher (much to the disgust of one of my French tutors, who judged this choice to be a waste of an Oxford education) and later went on to work in the Education Department of the National Gallery at a time of solid public funding, when we were able to make inventive and inclusive provision for our visitors. Along the way I also wrote, lectured, did – and still do – leadership training for the NHS and looked forward in the way that mid-career people do. I was probably being the 'best self' that Cornelia Connelly, nineteenth-century American-born founder of the schools and order, wrote about a century before the phrase became current again. It was only decades later that a chance connection with a Holy Child sister led to an offer to write a script for a short film about the life of Cornelia and I found myself revisiting and reflecting on my own education.

As I read Cornelia's name in the email from one of the sisters, a single unwelcome image came into my mind: that of a woman cradling a terribly burned toddler in her arms. And then the rest of the story, or as much as I knew of it: Cornelia, a wife and mother of several children, before her life changed absolutely and she became a nun. By now a mother of four grown-up children myself, I began to wonder differently about her story, and accepted the job.

My research into Cornelia's life and work led me along many paths, but the one that to my surprise affected me most was not in the end the painful story of Cornelia's marriage to the ambitious and unpredictable pastor Pierce Connelly and her significantly tragic experiences of motherhood. Rather it was reading about the liberal, arts-rich education system that Cornelia developed after, for reasons apparently outside her control, she found herself obliged to become a nun, and then going on herself to found a teaching order in England. I realised that I was reading about the principles behind my school education, which, I now saw, had been exceptional. The Holy Child nuns who taught me, and their predecessors, were far from the grim tormentors of the Magdalene laundries. Those who taught me were independent, many of them highly educated women, who offered a humane, broad and creative curriculum: the school week was punctuated with jewelled moments of self-expression. At Cavendish Square it was music, eurythmics (movement to music), drama and the multi-sensory side of Catholicism as expressed in the statues of saints in every classroom who, to the eyes of a six-year-old, at least, were dressed in gorgeous fabrics, as well as candle-lit, hymn singing processions on high feast days. At Mayfield it was the drama of the Live Crib when we wound through the village streets performing the Christmas story, with Mary on a donkey, a real baby in her arms, Joseph knocking on the door of the local pub to ask for a bed for the night. I was mysteriously moved by the great arch of the fourteenth-century chapel, took out every art book in the well-stocked library and taught myself to identify artists' styles by covering up the captions. The art studio too was a haven where we drew from life and sometimes played guitar. To my surprise the nuns taught us to waltz, whirling us around the room to the sound of a crackly record.

It must have been this exposure to the world of the arts that so profoundly affected the way I approached my own career as an educator. At the primary school in Paddington where I first taught a year-three class consisting largely of refugee children with no English, I often used the arts as a way of reaching them, helping them to feel safe and confident in the way my own experience had done for me. These were the things I reflected on as I researched the Cornelia short-film script.

Shortly after delivering that script, another chance meeting, this time at a cinema, brought me back into contact with author and playwright Diane Samuels (we had previously been neighbours). This unexpected encounter was the catalyst for the development of the play that has emerged as *Waltz with Me*. At that first meeting, my head was still full of Cornelia, so I passed her story on to Diane, and when we met again for a coffee I also mentioned by chance (but perhaps not?) a contemporary woman known to me whose situation, Diane later sensed, somehow mirrored Cornelia's. Diane asked me to join her in the research for the play and, thanks to the generosity of several supporters, we were able to follow Cornelia on some of her journeyings, from Philadelphia to Mayfield in Sussex, Derby and Alton Towers, Blackpool and Rome. We also got to know both Cornelia's spiritual descendants, the current Holy Child sisters, who always warmly welcomed and helped us, and the family of Cornelia's youngest son Frank, whose great-granddaughter Simonetta has the same gentle presence and fiery eyes as the ones we see in contemporary photographs of Cornelia.

Our period of research was punctuated with many more synchronistic, illuminating and delightful encounters of all kinds, so uncanny at times that we grew to put them down to Cornelia's intervention from wherever she is (there is, after all, a current application to the Vatican to make Cornelia Connelly a saint).

In the end it seems that I had unwittingly sparked Diane's talent for imaginative and empathetic invention, and in *Waltz with Me* she brings the stories of the two women together, giving them heightened life in an extraordinarily powerful way. Here Cornelia, previously in my mind little more than a victim of her circumstances, becomes the pragmatic, resolute and creative person that she must have been to achieve what she did – flawed, like the rest of us, but endlessly engaging.

With this publication we are hopeful that the women whose lives have inspired this story, separated by time but not circumstance, will find new life on the stage. Perhaps the play will also speak to many others who struggle to align personal lives and responsibilities with their heart's calling to play a role in the wider world, bearing losses incurred on the way by developing deeper understanding and generosity of action. At my Holy Child schools, I witnessed how Cornelia's curriculum demonstrated her belief in live performance as something that enhanced individual development and communal engagement, a notion that is definitely imbued in this script. I am grateful to Diane for many things, but especially for helping me re-evaluate my own education, a very rounding experience.

GHISLAINE KENYON
March 2023

CHARACTERS

Maggie Byrne — Modern day: lapsed Catholic, mother, educator, musician/composer

Cornelia Peacock Connelly — Nineteenth century: originally American, wife, mother, then nun/ Reverend Mother, educationalist, foundress of Society of the Holy Child Jesus order and schools (1809–79)

Pete/ Pierce Connelly — Modern day: Maggie's husband
Nineteenth century: Cornelia's husband, originally American, Episcopalian (Protestant) vicar converting to Catholicism and then back to the Episcopalian Church

Mike/ John Henry — Modern day: Maggie's lover/partner
Nineteenth century: Cornelia's toddler (second son)

Frank/ Bishop Wiseman/ Mr Harting — Cornelia's youngest (third) son
English Bishop
Solicitor

Merty/	Nineteenth century: Cornelia's eldest son
Luke/	Modern day: Maggie's son
(Violinist)	

Adeline (Ady)/	Nineteenth century: Cornelia's daughter
Gwendaline/	Cornelia's English friend
Iris	Modern day: Maggie's daughter
(Flautist)	

Sister Theodora/	Modern day: nun in her seventies
Sister Emily/	Nineteenth century: young nun
(Pianist)	

Instead of actor/musicians, a pianist, violinist and/or flautist of any age or gender may play separately from the acting company.

BIOGRAPHICAL INFO

Mercer (Merty): Cornelia and Pierce's eldest son (died at 20)

Adeline: Cornelia and Pierce's surviving daughter (died at 65)

John Henry: Cornelia and Pierce's second son (died at 3)

Mary Magdalen: Cornelia and Pierce's second daughter (died as a young baby)

Pierce Francis (Frank): Cornelia and Pierce's youngest son (died at 90)

Gwendaline: Daughter of the Earl of Shrewsbury, Catholic aristocrat, married to Prince Borghese in her early 20s

MUSIC

The following pieces have been selected to provide an example of the significant role music plays in the storytelling and drama.

For the reader, if you wish to be adventurous and add another dimension to your reading experience, you are invited to source the pieces that are publicly available and listen as you read. At the time of writing a streamable playlist has been created, containing the majority of the tunes below. You can find a link to this on the *Waltz With Me* page on the publisher's website (renardpress.com/books/waltz-with-me).

For those mounting a production, please see this list as a guide to the musical landscape and feel free, if preferred, to make your own choices.

'Musetta's Waltz' from *La bohème* by Puccini
'Waltz in F Major' by Verdi
'Waltz in A-Flat Major', Op. 69, No. 1 ('Adieu' waltz) by Chopin
'Little Maggie' by Old-Time bluegrass – travelling music
'Mary Had a Little Lamb', traditional children's song, , 'Little Lamp' variations
'Cow and Dogs and Horses', a playful, improvised nursery ditty – original composition
'Veni Creator Spiritus', plain chant, variations
'Panis Angelicus' by César Franck

'Oh My God, Trim Thy Vine', spiritual 'work song' – original
  composition
'Bells', original composition
'The Derby Ram', traditional folk song
'Sonata in E Major', Op. 1, No. 15 by Handel

For license to use original compositions of 'Cows and Dogs
and Horses', 'Oh My God, Trim Thy Vine' and 'Bells' by
David Osmond, please contact:
Mary Nelson at Nelson Browne Management ltd
48 Warwick Street, London W1B 5AW
Tel: 07796 891388
enquiries@nelsonbrowne.com

WALTZ WITH ME

The play is held across time and space
in a golden ballroom.

If a piano was playing when Mother Cornelia came into a room, she'd sweep up the nearest girl and waltz her off her feet.

'Cornelia was very fond, I think, of life, love, singing, all of that.'

SISTER JUDITH LANCASTER

'The remembrance of my children never leaves me.'

MOTHER CORNELIA CONNELLY

ACT I

BEST SELF

Golden light. A piano. Light shifts to grey day. Image of a tomb with memorial stone:

CORNELIA AUGUSTA CONNELLY 1809–1879
FOUNDRESS OF THE SOCIETY OF THE HOLY CHILD JESUS
LOVE KNOWETH NO MEASURE, FEARETH NO
LABOUR, MAKETH SWEET ALL THAT IS BITTER,
FINDETH REST IN GOD ALONE.

SISTER THEODORA *is at the piano playing 'Musetta's Waltz' from* La bohème. MAGGIE, *in her late thirties, appears in a nervous rush, heading for the piano.*

MAGGIE: Shit.

THEODORA: Back to the old chapel piano, Maggie?

MAGGIE: Oh God. Sorry, Sister Theodora.

THEODORA: Are you to play later?

MAGGIE: Not sure... Not ready... Sorry, seem to be falling short of... what was it... 'Be your good self...'?

THEODORA: 'Be your best self...'

MAGGIE: Right.

THEODORA: 'The self God wants you to be.'

MAGGIE: You know, I don't think I can play. Best not.

(MAGGIE *moves away from the piano.*)

23

MAGGIE: Don't want to spoil your celebration.

THEODORA: Well, I'm most touched you've made it.

MAGGIE: Of course, for your send-off.

THEODORA: How is it to be here again?

MAGGIE: Weren't the corridors longer... and colder? Everything seems... so... I dunno... familiar... yet different... like the new annexe out there... like those words that have appeared on the foundress's tomb.

THEODORA: You mean 'Love knoweth no measure...'? Cornelia's words have been there as long as she has.

MAGGIE: Not when I was here.

THEODORA: Certainly.

MAGGIE: But in my last year at Live Crib I sat right there with the real baby that wouldn't stop crying.

THEODORA: You played Joseph as a very attentive father.

MAGGIE: Desperate as hell... the infant Jesus howling... me praying with all my might, 'Please, please make it quiet'... to Mother Cornelia... I could have sworn... behind her blank tombstone.

THEODORA: To notice what's always there we tend to need to be ready.

MAGGIE: How ready?

THEODORA: Did the baby quieten?

MAGGIE: I think so... at some point.

THEODORA: The crying stays more in the memory, perhaps.

MAGGIE: Was it really half a lifetime ago?

THEODORA: Not of my life, to be sure.

MAGGIE: Do you mind retiring?

THEODORA: It's time.

MAGGIE: You'll be missed.

THEODORA: I'm glad to see so many of you again and provide the occasion for so much revisiting.

MAGGIE: Actually, I wanted the chance to say... Well, when I teach...

THEODORA: That's your work?

MAGGIE: Only part time. But it makes me realise how skilfully, invisibly, powerfully you enabled us to somehow come into our own when we had the barest sense of what that might be...

THEODORA: It works both ways, you know.

MAGGIE: Yes, yes, I learn incredibly from my students.

THEODORA: What do you teach?

MAGGIE: Music... playing... composition a bit... But the subject is merely the medium. It's really about whole person, isn't it?

THEODORA: Such is the Holy Child approach.

MAGGIE: 'Words not actions.'

THEODORA: 'Actions not words.'

MAGGIE: Sorry for being so out of touch. But your influence does prevail, I promise.

THEODORA: I should retire more often – it's rather gratifying.

MAGGIE: I wish I could play a piece you deserve.

THEODORA: Oh, since you've come all this way, why not play after all? I mean, what would you say to a student of yours?

MAGGIE: Well... I'd... I suppose... to... to just enjoy it...

THEODORA: How about a few turns to get you in the mood?

(THEODORA *starts playing Verdi's* 'Waltz in F Major'.)

MAGGIE: What, dance? Now? Beside the tomb?

THEODORA: Why not if it helps brighten the spirit?

MAGGIE: I've not done a waltz since school...

THEODORA: Come, now, step in time for Mother Cornelia in thanks for quieting the crying baby. Ready?

MAGGIE: Not at all.

THEODORA: Right foot back on One...

(*As* THEODORA *plays,* MAGGIE *tentatively tries to waltz.*)

MAGGIE: Left foot to the side on Two...

THEODORA: That's the way...

MAGGIE: Oh... I guess that after a couple of glasses of wine... I guess I could brace myself... To hell with it... I'll play.

THEODORA: Yes... the light fantastic toe.

(*The tomb opens. A figure emerges, wearing a nineteenth-century nun's habit.*)

CORNELIA: Oh, the light fantastic toe.

(CORNELIA *is about to start dancing too. Suddenly the chapel, the dancing, the music break.* PETE *appears.*)

PETE: Where did you stay?

MAGGIE: In a bed and breakfast.

PETE: On your own?

MAGGIE: Check it out if you like.

PETE: How was this school reunion, then?

MAGGIE: It was a retirement do.

PETE: Did you go to confession?

MAGGIE: Hardly.

PETE: No remorse?

MAGGIE: I told you. It's over.

PETE: So are you ready to tell me who he is?

MAGGIE: It wouldn't help.

PETE: Is it really over?

MAGGIE: What else am I meant to say?

PETE: If you see him again…

MAGGIE: Do you mind if I practise now?

PETE: Practise?

MAGGIE: Chopin's 'Waltz in A-Flat Major', opus 69, number 1.

PETE: Why?

MAGGIE: Because sad music makes me feel better.

(MAGGIE *starts playing Chopin's 'Adieu' waltz.*)

PETE: Because you miss him?

MAGGIE: Please can I just play?

PETE: You didn't answer my question.

MAGGIE: I need to play.

PETE: Is that right?

MAGGIE: I'm trying my best.

PETE: Are you?

(PETE *goes.* MAGGIE *continues playing, finding flow. Getting emotional, she stops. She finds her phone. She sends a text.*)

MAGGIE: How is this… in any way… my best bloody self?!

(MAGGIE*'s phone rings.*)

1

FIRST STEPS

The Liberty Bell rings. Golden light reveals the fullness of the shimmering ballroom space. Chopin's 'Adieu' waltz plays on piano. CORNELIA, *early twenties, appears and starts to pace out a waltz.*

CORNELIA: Right foot back on One. Left foot to the side on Two...

(Dappled sunlight through leaves. Birds sing. MAGGIE *arrives in a wood.)*

MAGGIE: Let me be sensible...
CORNELIA: Let me be at my very best...
MAGGIE: Let me do the right thing...

*(*MAGGIE *glances warily behind her, then waits.* CORNELIA *finds some flow in the waltz, spinning around, in another world, yet somehow tuning into* MAGGIE *'s.)*

CORNELIA: Right foot back on One. Left foot to the side on Two... Close together on Three. Right foot down...

(PIERCE *appears and surveys the space watchfully.* CORNELIA *swirls a swirl and bursts out laughing, bringing to life a soirée in a well-to-do house in Philadelphia in the early nineteenth century.*)

PIERCE: You seem to be enjoying yourself, Miss Peacock.
CORNELIA: I dare say I am, Mr Connelly.
PIERCE: Despite this music?
CORNELIA: Don't you like it?
PIERCE: Don't you find it rather melancholy?
CORNELIA: It ought to be – it's called 'Farewell'.
PIERCE: I'd rather listen to something happier.
CORNELIA: But the beauty of sad music is the happy thing.

(*The 'Adieu' waltz hangs in the air, then dissolves. Silence.* MIKE *appears.*)

MIKE: Hey.
MAGGIE: Hey.

(CORNELIA *laughs again.*)

PIERCE: My, you laugh a good deal.
CORNELIA: Do you mind it?
PIERCE: Such *joie de vivre* – dare I say passion – is hard to ignore.
CORNELIA: Is it, sir?
PIERCE: You certainly brighten the church when you sing.
CORNELIA: You can't possibly distinguish my voice from the rest of the choir.
PIERCE: The way your face blazes. Your song rises above them all. How could I not hear such fervour?

29

(*Birds sing.* MIKE *approaches* MAGGIE.)

MIKE: Are you sure you're OK with this?

MAGGIE: We can just… say hello… catch up, at least…

MIKE: Aren't we meant to be having no contact of any kind?

MAGGIE: We've been trying, haven't we… We have tried…

MIKE: Are you sure he still doesn't know it's me?

MAGGIE: Oh God, you know you'd know if he did.

MIKE: I have seen him… at a couple of law-society things…

MAGGIE: And?

MIKE: Perfectly civil… friendly…

MAGGIE: I'd better not stay long today.

MIKE: So… we're just saying hello…?

MAGGIE: Yes.

MIKE: That's all.

MAGGIE: Yes.

(CORNELIA *giggles.*)

PIERCE: You must notice me looking at you.

CORNELIA: Oughtn't you be attending to your duties?

PIERCE: Oh, the menial tasks of a curate are hardly taxing.

CORNELIA: Do you like to waltz, Mr Connelly?

PIERCE: Waltzing, Miss Peacock? Is that not rather… risqué?

CORNELIA: My sister and her reverend husband would not approve, I'm sure.

PIERCE: And is this because of the waltz or my meagre income?

CORNELIA: I do not care.

PIERCE: About their views or my standing?

CORNELIA: I see your qualities shine full of promise.

PIERCE: And a man who devotes himself to his true vocation with all his might must surely rise to his highest destiny.

CORNELIA: Now you are the one ablaze, sir.

PIERCE: How could I not like to waltz with you as my partner?

(PIERCE *steps confidently towards* CORNELIA. *She almost gasps with delight.* MAGGIE *and* MIKE *step closer.*)

MIKE: How have you been?

MAGGIE: Walking on eggshells.

MIKE: And now?

MAGGIE: I can breathe again… for a few hours, at least…

MIKE: Breathing's pretty crucial…

MAGGIE: It is.

MIKE: Essential, in fact.

MAGGIE: It really is.

(MIKE *and* MAGGIE *kiss passionately.* PIERCE *offers his hand to* CORNELIA.)

PIERCE: Will you join me, Miss Peacock?

CORNELIA: Thank you so much for asking, Mr Connelly.

(CORNELIA *takes* PIERCE*'s hand.* MAGGIE *and* MIKE *hold each other.*)

MIKE: We need to move on, love…

MAGGIE: I wish I knew how…

MIKE: I've been invited to be a founding partner in a new firm…

MAGGIE: Where?
MIKE: Not here.
MAGGIE: Where?
MIKE: Down south.

(PIERCE *and* CORNELIA *come closer.*)

PIERCE: Please... Let us continue, Cornelia...
CORNELIA: I never want this to end, Pierce...
PIERCE: Be with me for a lifetime of dances.
CORNELIA: Yes.
PIERCE: Remember the Scripture: 'Simply let your yes be a
    yes, and your no be a no.'
CORNELIA: Yes.

(CORNELIA *and* PIERCE *take up the hold for a waltz. The 'Adieu'*
waltz resumes.)

PIERCE: 'A man shall leave his father and mother.'
CORNELIA: 'And hold fast to his wife.'
PIERCE: 'And the two shall become...'
CORNELIA/PIERCE: '...one flesh.'

(MAGGIE *and* MIKE *hold each other.*)

MIKE: Come with me.
MAGGIE: Luke is only six, Mike... and Iris needs me... she's
    about to go to secondary... You can't ask me to do this.
MIKE: I can't not ask you.
MAGGIE: You mean... Be selfish... Is that what you're
    saying?

MIKE: Be honest.

MAGGIE: How can I?

MIKE: This is a real opportunity.

MAGGIE: Please don't go.

(CORNELIA *and* PIERCE *dance as they speak in graceful accord.*)

PIERCE: I take thee Cornelia Augusta Peacock to be my wedded wife...

CORNELIA: I take thee Pierce Connelly to be my wedded husband...

PIERCE/CORNELIA: ...to have and to hold from this day forward...

PIERCE: ...for better, for worse, for richer, for poorer...

CORNELIA: ...in sickness and in health...

PIERCE: ...to love and to cherish, till death us do part...

CORNELIA: ...according to God's holy ordinance...

CORNELIA/PIERCE: ...understanding that marriage is a lifelong union...

CORNELIA: ...and not to be entered into lightly.

PIERCE: For the purpose of mutual fellowship...

CORNELIA: ...for the procreation of children...

PIERCE: ...and their physical and spiritual nurture.

CORNELIA: I hereby give myself to you with my sacred vow before God...

PIERCE/CORNELIA: ...and thereto I plight thee my troth.

(*Silence.*)

33

MIKE: Maggie, we've started something. We can't un-start it. We've tried to say goodbye. But here we are. So either we get on with it… or what? What else…? And haven't you encouraged me to spread my wings? So, I am going away. And if you're not ready… not yet… I get that. Do what you need to do. Do what you really honestly need to do. I hope you'll join me. Take the time it takes. I mean it. There's no schedule, no requirement. I'm not going to stop loving you. No measure, love. No limits.

(*As dusk falls,* MAGGIE *and* MIKE *kiss again. Then he goes.* PIERCE *holds up a wedding ring for all to see.*)

PIERCE/CORNELIA: Bless, O Lord, this ring…

PIERCE: …that he who gives it…

CORNELIA: …and she who wears it…

PIERCE/CORNELIA: …may abide in thy peace, and continue in thy favour…

CORNELIA: …unto their life's end.

MAGGIE: Is this how it ends?

(PIERCE *places the ring on to the fourth finger of* CORNELIA*'s left hand.*)

PIERCE: With this ring, I thee wed: in the name of the Father, and of the Son, and of the Holy Ghost.

(*Bells peal. Dusk softens into darkness.* THEODORA *joins* MAGGIE.)

MAGGIE: Oh, Sister Theodora, I really didn't expect you to come to meet me here.

THEODORA: Your call coincided perfectly with my Blackpool trip.

MAGGIE: It's still out of your way…

THEODORA: Arrangements have conspired in our favour, Maggie. Let's trust that. How are you?

MAGGIE: Like I said, I don't want to do the wrong thing.

THEODORA: Have you asked him again to consider counselling?

MAGGIE: He absolutely won't.

THEODORA: I see you're aware that marriage is sacred and for ever.

MAGGIE: We didn't marry in a church.

THEODORA: You have two children.

MAGGIE: We do.

THEODORA: So what else do you think I might suggest?

MAGGIE: That I've made my bed and lie in it?

THEODORA: Simply that?

MAGGIE: What else?

THEODORA: What else is there?

MAGGIE: You mean pray?

THEODORA: It's an option.

MAGGIE: My praying's even rustier than my playing.

THEODORA: You ended up playing most vividly at my retirement, didn't you?

MAGGIE: Can we just sit together?

THEODORA: We can.

(*They sit silently.*)

MAGGIE: I want to make a promise. Will you hear it?

THEODORA: I'm listening.

MAGGIE: I promise… to devote myself… give my absolute all… to facing this… to following what my heart and every cell of my being is urging me to do… even if there is great fault on my part…

(*Silence.*)

MAGGIE: Are you still listening?
THEODORA: I am.
MAGGIE: I promise… to do everything I possibly can… to protect my children from bearing the brunt of my actions. I promise to trust my love for them to guide me. And their father… whatever he might do… to be brave enough… Yes, I will brave it somehow. I promise to find a way… to rise above my failing… and from now on to be as true as humanly possible… true to myself… to Iris… to Luke… to Pete, too… I can't live with him any more… He can't stand living with me… We have to face the truth… And act on it.
THEODORA: Is there anything else, Maggie?

(MAGGIE *removes the wedding ring from the fourth finger of her left hand.*)

MAGGIE: Amen?

2

NEW HORIZONS

Late night.

PETE (*off*): I'm going to bed now. And in the morning, Maggie, when I wake up, you won't be here. Do you understand? You will get your lying, deceiving presence out of the home you have no right to live in. You will be gone.

(CORNELIA *is in the bedroom she and* PIERCE *share at her sister's home in Philadelphia, preparing for bed.* PIERCE *appears, holding a burning candle.*)

PIERCE: What's that look?
CORNELIA: It's the look of the luckiest woman in the world, ready for the best husband I could ever hope for.
PIERCE: Close those searching eyes, please, whilst I undress.

(CORNELIA *closes her eyes.*)

PIERCE: Are you peeping?
CORNELIA: Not at all.

(*He is silent. She listens and senses.* MAGGIE *gets a small case and, shaking, crams what she needs into it.*)

MAGGIE: OK, OK... What else... What else...?
CORNELIA: I know you're still there.

(PIERCE *comes closer.*)

CORNELIA: Ahhhh... I can hear the beating of your heart...
    where a little drummer boy stands to perfect attention.
PIERCE: You can even see into my heart?
CORNELIA: And into the smallest recesses of your mind...
    where all your thoughts vie with one another.
PIERCE: I had no idea that my wife had such remarkable
    insight.
CORNELIA: You're the one who inspires it.
PIERCE: And what else can you tell me of my thoughts?
CORNELIA: They are impatient... searching...
PIERCE: What if they're racing ahead of you?
CORNELIA: Racing where?
PIERCE: How far can this vision of yours stretch?

(*He kisses her passionately. A small lamp is glowing. Under duvets,
sleeping, are* LUKE *and* IRIS. MAGGIE *tries to calm her agitated state
and whispers.*)

MAGGIE: Oh, God, I wish I could take you with me... But
    you're better off sleeping now... I'm going to have to
    make arrangements... I will... Then I'll get you...

(CORNELIA, *alert, looks into* PIERCE*'s eyes.*)

CORNELIA: Do you have something to tell me?
PIERCE: I intend to resign my position as curate...

CORNELIA: I did wonder if you were making some secret plans.

PIERCE: Well, they have proved to be fruitful... I am soon to become a rector, my dear, with a parish of my very own.

CORNELIA: Oh, Pierce, where?

PIERCE: We must travel some distance...

CORNELIA: How far?

PIERCE: Mississippi.

CORNELIA: All the way to Mississippi?

(MAGGIE *produces two new toothbrushes and a note addressed to* IRIS.)

MAGGIE: OK, Iris, these are the ones the dentist gave us... Just remember to remind Lukie over the next few days about brushing teeth.... And red and green are as good as each other, so whichever you get is fine. I'm leaving them right here... here... so you'll find them...

(*She puts the toothbrushes beside* IRIS.)

CORNELIA: Must we leave our families behind?

PIERCE: This is for my betterment... for our betterment, little homebody.

CORNELIA: I dare say... Of course it is.

(CORNELIA *puts her arms around* PIERCE *and kisses him.* MAGGIE *holds two tubes of sun cream.*)

MAGGIE: Here's the factor-fifty for when you're at the park and playing out. (*She holds two sun hats.*) Sun hats. Wear them. (*She puts the sun cream and hats between the two children. She kisses her hand and places it on her daughter's head.*) I'll phone. See you soon.

(*'Little Maggie' plays.*)

PIERCE: Forwards, Nelie…

CORNELIA: Well, if you are to become a rector… then I shall bear… in good grace… as best I can… all the upheaval and so very much travelling.

PIERCE: That's the spirit.

(CORNELIA *looks up. She stares up and up. She reaches up.*)

CORNELIA: Now I see a ladder.

PIERCE: How high does it reach?

CORNELIA: Higher than the highest steeple… Higher still…

(*Music suspends, tensely.* MAGGIE *has a child-size violin case. She places it beside her sleeping son.*)

MAGGIE: Here you are, for your lesson tomorrow, Lukie. See you sooner than soon, love.

(*She kisses her hand and places it on her son's head.* PIERCE *suddenly sweeps* CORNELIA *off her feet and into his arms.*)

PIERCE: Off we go!

(MAGGIE *pulls herself away from her children, back to her case. 'Little Maggie' resumes with gusto.*)

PIERCE: Keep up, little one…
CORNELIA: I'm here…

(PIERCE *swirls* CORNELIA *in a fine dance. She is lost in his whirl.* MAGGIE *zips her case closed.*)

PIERCE: Out of Philadelphia, on to Pittsburgh… all the way down the Ohio River, through West Virginia, Kentucky… Tennessee… and on to Mississippi… and Natchez.
CORNELIA: Is this it?

(MAGGIE *picks up her case.*)

PIERCE: Look up. See. Where the land rises – those two oak trees.
CORNELIA: Beside the white-frame house?

(*Silence.*)

PIERCE: How do you like our new home?

(MAGGIE *reaches out towards the glowing lamp.*)

MAGGIE: No going back.

(*In the dimness, there is a sense of loss so suddenly strong that time distorts.* CORNELIA, *a vision of herself yet to come, coughs. Violin hauntingly accompanies.*)

CORNELIA: Not lamb... silly... little lamp...
    (*singing*): Little lamp... little lamp...
    Mary had a little lamp... She followed it about.
    And then one day the cool breeze blew...
    Cool breeze blew... cool breeze blew...
    Then one day the cold breeze blew...
    And blew the lamp right...

(MAGGIE *switches off the light.*)

3

WHITE COTTAGE

Violinist, like a child learning, repeats over and over a simple accompaniment for 'Mary Had a Little Lamb'.

MAGGIE (*on phone*): Hey, Luke…

(*Violinist starts to lose concentration.*)

MAGGIE (*on phone*): Guess what you can see from my window where I'm living right now…? Can you hear…? It's the sea… and up the beach are huts, all different colours… and a brilliant fish-and-chip place down the road… You'll love it…

(*Violinist stops playing.*)

MAGGIE: Darling, remember, if Daddy gets cross, it's nothing you've done.… Don't let him upset you… It'll be OK… I'll make sure it's OK… I promise.

(CORNELIA *is pregnant. She carries a white toy cottage and pulls out toy farmyard animals, laying them around it.*)

CORNELIA (*singing*): Lambs and cows and dogs and horses…
Pigs and dogs and cows and sheep…

(MERTY, CORNELIA *and* PIERCE*'s eldest son, currently not quite two years old, picks up a sheep.*)

CORNELIA (*singing*): So, Merty, what does the sheep say?

(MERTY *makes a moo.*)

CORNELIA (*singing*): Oh, Merty, what does the sheep say?

(MERTY *makes a bigger moo.* MAGGIE *has a book of violin music for children.*)

MAGGIE (*on phone*): Oh Lukey… How's your violin practice…? Look, if it's hard to find help at home now, you can always ask your teacher… And let me know if you need anything else… I've got some new music for you… I'll be with you again for teatime tomorrow…

(CORNELIA *picks up a cow.*)

CORNELIA (*singing*): So, Merty, what does the cow say?

(MERTY *makes a neigh.*)

CORNELIA (*singing*): Come, Merty, what does the cow say?

(MERTY *makes a neigh.*)

CORNELIA (*singing*): Is that really what the cow says?

(MERTY *laughs and neighs again.*)

CORNELIA (*singing*): Now, now, what does the cow really say?

(MERTY *makes a moo sound.*)

CORNELIA: Bravo, Master Connelly!

(MERTY *neighs again.* PIERCE *joins them. He picks up a dog.*)

PIERCE: Don't you like dogs best, Merty?
MERTY: Woof woof!
PIERCE: Woof woof woof.
MERTY: Woof woof woof woof woof woof!

(PIERCE *points to a bunch of animals lying a way away.*)

PIERCE: What are all those animals doing over there…?
    Quick, before they run away. Quick, quick!

(MERTY *races after the errant animals.*)

CORNELIA (*singing*): Hear the horses neigh neigh neigh,
    Hear the dogs go woof woof woof,
    Hear the cows…
PIERCE: Nelie? Have you been introducing Sallie and
    Phoebe to the alphabet?
CORNELIA: They're doing so well.
PIERCE: Education is not for slaves.

45

CORNELIA: But when he placed them here, the good doctor said to treat them as family.

PIERCE: I am noticed, Nelie. The Bishop has commended my 'faithful labours' as a 'most ardent high churchman.'

CORNELIA: Then advancement can only be a matter of time.

PIERCE: So, my love, please refrain from any well-meant but misguided actions that compromise our good standing.

CORNELIA: Oh… then… I guess… I shall do my best.

(MAGGIE *holds a school prospectus and reads the motto from it.*)

MAGGIE: Actions not words.

(MERTY *returns with handfuls of animals.*)

MERTY: Mama! Papa!

CORNELIA: Oh, look at all these creatures you've rescued!

(MERTY *moos.* PIERCE *moos.* CORNELIA *moos.* PIERCE *becomes* PETE.)

PETE: Forget it.

MAGGIE: But mediation—

PETE: Waste of time.

MAGGIE: I'm not asking for sole custody—

PETE: You won't be getting any kind of custody.

MAGGIE: I've admitted… I admit…

PETE: Adultery… abandonment… anything else?

MAGGIE: Come on, Pete, please…

PETE: If you have anything to discuss from now on, do it through your lawyer.

MAGGIE: This is between you and me. We're the ones who made this family, built this home together—

PETE: And you're the one who shat on it.

MAGGIE: We must work this through, for the children, at least…

PETE: Have you been practicing this little speech with Mike?

MAGGIE: He's tried to contact you.

PETE: He was supposed to be my friend.

MAGGIE: It's not his fault that you and I grew so apart.

PETE: Don't turn it back on me… You… you… Sneaking around, plotting… Why the hell did you give Iris that prospectus behind my back?

MAGGIE: She asked about my old school.

PETE: What, to be indoctrinated on the other side of the country?

MAGGIE: It's not like that… Don't shut down her options.

PETE: They both need stability right now.

MAGGIE: Look, I know this isn't easy—

PETE: No, Maggie, it's not going to be easy… I promise, in fact, that it's going to be very, very difficult for you… more difficult than you can possibly imagine.

MAGGIE: Who's always looked after them most of the time?

PETE: It takes more than appointments at the dentist, tubes of sun cream and packed lunches to be a decent bloody mother.

MAGGIE: You have no idea what it takes every day. And I can prove it. I will prove it.

(MERTY *approaches with a dog in one hand and a horse in the other.*)

MERTY: Woof woof!

(PETE *is now* PIERCE *again.*)

PIERCE: Woof woof woof.
MERTY: Woof woof woof woof woof woof!
CORNELIA (*singing*): Dogs and sheep and dogs and cows,
    Pigs and sheep and dogs and horses...
    What do all the horses say?

(MERTY *makes a moo.*)

CORNELIA (*singing*): What do those galloping horses say?

(MERTY *makes a baa.*)

CORNELIA (*singing*): Every single horse, it says...

(MERTY *neighs and neighs.*)

CORNELIA (*singing*): Hear the horses neigh neigh NEIGH!
PIERCE: One day, Master Mercer Connelly, you shall ride a
    horse. And go wherever you wish – over hedges, across
    fields, to the other side of the hills and far beyond.

(MERTY *oinks.*)

PIERCE: However, it is quite impossible to ride a pig
    anywhere.
CORNELIA: Oh, but nothing could stop you riding whatever
    you like, if you really feel it matters.

48

PIERCE: With you behind me, Nelie, I could ride even a pig
to the very top of the cathedral spire.
CORNELIA: Let's rise above even the spire.

(PIERCE *looks up*.)

4

FAITH

Wind blows, sea swells, gulls squawk. MIKE, *wearing coat and hat, relishes the elements.*

MIKE: Ready for these viewings?

(MAGGIE *wraps up warm.*)

MAGGIE: How far?
MIKE: Two in Hastings, two in St Leonards.
MAGGIE: St Leonards?
MIKE: Near the seafront.
MAGGIE: That's funny... I think the original convent – the one founded before my old school – might be there...
MIKE: Do you know where, exactly?
MAGGIE: Can we look it up... if we have time?

(*They head off.* CORNELIA*'s pregnancy is nearing term. She sits at the piano practising, learning the 'Adieu' waltz.* PIERCE, *troubled, paces. He clutches a handful of pamphlets.*)

PIERCE: Tell me, Nelie: ought I to be preaching more widely?
CORNELIA: Pierce, please let me practise.
PIERCE: This is a matter of urgency.

CORNELIA: I promised to play at the doctor's next week after dinner.

PIERCE: Ought I to take on extra duties, travel further afield?

CORNELIA: You already travel a good deal.

(CORNELIA *practises;* PIERCE *paces.*)

PIERCE: Might I have ministered a single baptism, wedding or funeral with more devotion?

CORNELIA: Dear one, your piety cannot be questioned.

PIERCE: So how do you explain my lack of progress?

CORNELIA: Come now! Your congregation has swelled.

PIERCE: Why, then, am I overlooked?

CORNELIA: Trust, as I do, that when the moment is right you will be granted the authority of Bishop.

PIERCE: But what if I remain a rector – mere little foot-soldier – for the rest of my God-given life?

CORNELIA: Patience, now. Practise, persevere and persist.

PIERCE: Our Church, Nelie, is failing us in more ways than one.

(PIERCE *waves the pamphlets.* CORNELIA *gives up her practising*)

PIERCE: Look at what they're distributing. Listen to this: 'Beware the dire, ignorant, migrant hordes… swarm upon superstitious swarm… with their devilish Catholic creed…' As a man of the cloth, how can I possibly be contaminated by this appalling viciousness against another Church?

CORNELIA: Rise above it.

PIERCE: By my honour, I can barely hold up my head… never mind bear to give my sacred service…

CORNELIA: Simply continue to give the best of yourself…

PIERCE: Do you not see? My confidence is leaving me. My faith in the Episcopalian establishment… the very core of my faith… is breaking.

CORNELIA: Darling, we cannot be inspired by our frustrations.

PIERCE: What am I to do when my path of devotion is turning to rubble?

CORNELIA: Might you seek an advisor… some guidance?

PIERCE: As it happens, I have been raising my concerns with our Catholic friend the Monseigneur…

CORNELIA: Well, there you are – if anyone disproves that base propaganda against his faith, he does. No one we know is less 'ignorant' or 'superstitious'.

PIERCE: And he appreciates my qualities… highly values our discussions. Most highly!

(*Silence.*)

PIERCE: There's no doubt; I must examine my conscience.

CORNELIA: In the true spirit of God, Pierce.

PIERCE: Words are insufficient, Nelie. I must take action.

CORNELIA: Let us pray, my love. Together.

(*They kneel beside each other in prayer. Silence. Water drips.* MAGGIE *and* MIKE *in the chapel, in poor repair, of the convent at St Leonards.*)

MIKE: The caretaker was right about the water damage.

MAGGIE: Good acoustic.

MIKE: Pews aren't in too bad condition.

MAGGIE: D'you ever miss going to church?

MIKE: Can't be doing with the cant.

MAGGIE: Is that why we both married atheists?

MIKE: To make our escape.

MAGGIE: I find that's not really my way either.

MIKE: You have a searching soul, my love.

MAGGIE: And you?

MIKE: Infinity is there, whether we see it or not. Why try to name the unnameable?

MAGGIE: It's peaceful here, isn't it?

MIKE: He said we can look around the classrooms too.

MAGGIE: How about we sit first… for a little while?

(Water drips. They sit beside each other quietly.)

PIERCE *(singing)*: *Veni, Creator Spiritus,*
  Mentes tuorum visita,
  Imple superna gratia
  Quae tu creasti pectora.

  (Come, Holy Ghost, Creator blest,
  And in our hearts take up Thy rest;
  Come with Thy grace and heav'nly aid
  To fill the hearts which Thou hast made.)

PIERCE: Are you listening?

CORNELIA: Yes. I hear.

PIERCE: So European, so learned. So ancient and glorious.

CORNELIA: Perhaps the Episcopalian Church attacks the Catholic Church because it poses a real threat.

PIERCE: What if the Catholic Church truly is the only univer-
sal Church?
(Sings) *Qui diceris Paraclitus*
Altissimi donum Dei,
Fons vivus, ignis, caritas,
Et spiritalis unctio.

(*To Thee, the Comforter, we cry,*
To Thee, the Gift of God most high,
The Fount of life, the Fire of love,
The soul's anointing from above.)

(CORNELIA *joins in singing 'Veni Creator Spiritus'.*)

PIERCE/CORNELIA (*singing*): *Deo Patri sit gloria,*
Et Filio qui a mortuis
Surrexit, ac Paraclito
In saeculorum saecula.

(*Praise we the Father and the Son*
And Holy Spirit, with them One;
And may the Son on us bestow
The gifts that from the Spirit flow.)

(*A bell rings three tolls. The knell transports* CORNELIA. *Suddenly older, alone, she clasps her hands.*)

CORNELIA: Oh, Mother of Sorrows…
MAGGIE: Is that the chapel bell?
MIKE: How can it be?
MAGGIE: Is there even a bell still up there?

MIKE: No one to ring it.

MAGGIE: Maybe the Holy Spirit wants to call us back into the faith.

(MAGGIE *and* MIKE *fall into silence again.*)

CORNELIA: ...Mother of Sorrows... Do you again reveal to me what you bear?

(MAGGIE *takes* MIKE's *hand.*)

MAGGIE: What are you thinking?

MIKE: About the houses we've seen... about this being a good place to settle. You?

MAGGIE: About the divorce... my chances in court...

MIKE: It's wise to be realistic.

MAGGIE: You're not hopeful?

MIKE: You did leave the family home, love.

MAGGIE: As an emergency measure.

MIKE: He knows how to exploit it.

MAGGIE: Does it have to come to this between us?

MIKE: You've known him long enough.

MAGGIE: But he wasn't always... You've seen how charming he can be when he wants to be... and dynamic... damn clever...

MIKE: I'm not accusing you of being a poor judge of character.

MAGGIE: OK, I admit I mistook his single-mindedness for true authority... kidded myself that his fire was keeping me warm... If I'm honest, I needed his spark... like he needed my grounding... Only more and more it's been like living with a volcano... flaring and rupturing... all the foundations melting beneath us.

55

MIKE: I'm sorry for my part in the way we've handled this.

MAGGIE: Stop being guilty.

MIKE: We find ourselves in a chapel. What do you expect?

MAGGIE: Don't you find any solace in this silence?

MIKE: Isn't silence anywhere if you listen?

MAGGIE: But in lapsing, you do still lose something precious.

MIKE: Like?

MAGGIE: Like the music.

MIKE: Yes, the Church does bloody good music.

MAGGIE: I've lost even the most simple and plain.

(ADELINE *appears and cries some baby cries.* CORNELIA *holds her newborn in her arms, soothing. Her daughter settles.*)

PIERCE: Adeline, you say?

CORNELIA: After my sister. Doesn't it suit her?

(PIERCE *kisses his baby, then his wife on the forehead.*)

PIERCE: Dear little Adeline, you arrive at a most significant time. Darling daughter, your father must have some higher power to be obeyed, whose authority can be trusted. I realise that in Saint Peter alone and his successors has this divine right been invested. And so, Ady, dearest Nelie, I have decided to enter the Catholic Church.

CORNELIA: What about your vocation as a minister?

PIERCE: Sacrifices must be made to follow the holy path. I am content to step down from priestly office and be no more than a simple layman in the congregation bowing to the one true faith. I hope that I can rely upon your full support.

CORNELIA: But must we leave our White Cottage, our twin
oak trees, all our friends?

PIERCE: Are you not ready fully to embrace the Catholic
faith too? Let us now bind on our sandals.

CORNELIA: Where will we go?

PIERCE: As pilgrims in search of truth, Nelie, all paths lead
to one place alone.

CORNELIA: How far?

PIERCE: All the way to Rome.

(*'Veni Creator Spiritus' plays.*)

5

CONFESS

THEODORA *clasps* MAGGIE*'s hands.*

THEODORA: Terrific presentation.

MAGGIE: Did the sisters enjoy it?

THEODORA: You have something with this new piano method of yours.

MAGGIE: Do you think so?

THEODORA: And you've been invited to the Holy Child School in Ghana…

MAGGIE: I really want to go…

THEODORA: How are you getting on otherwise?

MAGGIE: Oh… Visiting rights. That's all the court has granted me.

THEODORA: That must be disappointing.

MAGGIE: I'm appealing.

THEODORA: Is that going to help?

MAGGIE: I can provide a stable, loving home now. I'll prove it.

THEODORA: How are you settling in?

MAGGIE: Living by the sea is such a tonic.

THEODORA: St Leonards is one place I find Cornelia to be most present. Not everyone does. But I do.

MAGGIE: I take myself into the old chapel some days… after a walk… to clear my mind… find perspective…

(THEODORA *hands* MAGGIE *a book.*)

THEODORA: I hope this may be of interest, in part by way of a thank you for being involved in our conference today, and somehow continuing Cornelia's work by uniquely developing your own, in the spirit of hers, if you don't mind my saying so – you could say furthering it…

MAGGIE: I didn't know you'd written about her.

THEODORA: My small contribution to the question of sainthood.

MAGGIE: Is Mother Connelly a saint?

THEODORA: She's officially venerable, which is a start. And if anyone's prayer to intercede for divine help leads to a proven miracle, then she'll become beatified, Blessed.

MAGGIE: And for sainthood, another miracle?

THEODORA: A second miracle. Yes.

MAGGIE: Have you known any prayers to Cornelia to lead to a miracle?

THEODORA: I dare say.

MAGGIE: How on earth do you prove such a thing?

(*'Veni Creator Spiritus' plays.* CORNELIA, *dressed for travel, is shaking with fear.*)

CORNELIA: How vast is that ocean out there? What storms, what perils of the deep might swallow us? What if we never reach Rome? Dear God, I am not ready to meet you.

(*Harmonics become discordant.*)

CORNELIA: Here, now, in New Orleans, dear Lord, let me enter your grand cathedral of white. Let me kneel before you and by communion be received entirely into the true Catholic Church.

(MAGGIE *opens a bottle of wine.*)

CORNELIA: How do I start afresh in all innocence, as my babes, trusting to whatever lies in store?

(MAGGIE *pours herself a glass of wine. Wind blows.*)

CORNELIA: Let me be ready.

(*Wind blows.*)

CORNELIA: Take strength. Find courage to face the swell. The voyage must be made. So let me be cleansed of all blemish. Let me, dear God, be baptised.

(*Silence.* CORNELIA *kneels in Confession.* MAGGIE *raises her glass.*)

CORNELIA: I confess to giving into weakness... to losing heart...
MAGGIE: Here's to... not losing heart...
CORNELIA: ...to wanting to hold on to material comfort...
MAGGIE: ...to no regrets...
CORNELIA: ...to allowing nightmares to overtake me...
MAGGIE: ...to looking ahead...
CORNELIA: ...to dwelling upon difficulties...
MAGGIE: ...to hanging on in there...

CORNELIA: ...to giving way to sadness and tears, mistrust...
losing faith...

MAGGIE: ...to making this damn situation bloody work...

CORNELIA: ...to giving into dread and mortal terror.

MAGGIE: OK, Cornelia, I'm asking... I'm praying with
every breath in my body... for a miracle... Please...
please, please... make Pete drop down dead... stone
cold dead.

CORNELIA: Oh my God, I am sorry, with all my heart.

MAGGIE: Why be sorry for making mistakes and being
flawed and taking risks and following your bloody heart?
Don't be sorry. Learn. Just damn well learn.

(MAGGIE *downs the glass of wine in one.*)

6

VOYAGE

Wind blows. Ocean surges. Up on deck, PIERCE *takes in the sea air and looks up to the night sky.*

PIERCE: Sacrifices are required to live a holy life. But for those devoted and courageous enough to aspire to ascend the ladder, all difficulties are but glorious rewards.

(MIKE *appears with a box.* MAGGIE *joins him.*)

MIKE: So, is this the kind of thing you played with when you were little, on your own, with no one else in charge?
MAGGIE: Because?
MIKE: That's what I'm led to believe reveals what a person is about – what your thing in life truly is.

(MAGGIE *looks inside the box.*)

MAGGIE: Hmmm.

(MAGGIE *takes out pieces of a glockenspiel.*)

MIKE: I hope it's all there.

(MAGGIE *starts to set up the glockenspiel.*)

MAGGIE: Yep, this is like being a kid again.

MIKE: Have some fun.

MAGGIE: Do I deserve any fun?

MIKE: Probably not. But what the hell.

(MIKE *leaves her to it.* CORNELIA *approaches* PIERCE.)

PIERCE: There you are.

CORNELIA: The little ducklings are sleeping at last.

PIERCE: Is the nurse looking over them?

CORNELIA: If she feels so inclined.

PIERCE: Now, now.

CORNELIA: She's such a fussy goose. If only we could tip her quietly overboard.

PIERCE: Nelie!

CORNELIA: Another baby would be easier.

PIERCE: Already?

CORNELIA: When they're fast asleep, the thought is tempting.

PIERCE: So, she managed to settle them to bed?

CORNELIA: I sang to them. She groaned. Then I offered her some bread and she complained it wasn't fresh.

(CORNELIA *takes some dry bread out of her pocket and gives* PIERCE *a piece.* MAGGIE *strikes the glockenspiel. It rings. She plays, interweaving/counterpointing* PIERCE *and* CORNELIA*'s conversation.*)

PIERCE: It could be fresher.

CORNELIA: Stale is best for settling seasickness.

PIERCE: And yet, my dear, you're looking a little heartier these days.

CORNELIA: Am I? Maybe it's these bracing seas.

PIERCE: So the voyage is not so utterly intolerable. See.

(MAGGIE *plays tick-tock time-passing notes…*)

CORNELIA: Fourteen days, twenty hours and six minutes.

PIERCE: And with each second you become not only stronger, my delicate flower, but even more beautiful.

CORNELIA: Promise me that Marseilles is somewhere out there.

PIERCE: We'll arrive soon enough.

CORNELIA: Oh, to wash again.

(MAGGIE *tries different bell-like sounds…*)

MAGGIE: That chapel bell… ringing from nowhere…

(MAGGIE *improvises bell-like sequences.* PIERCE *puts his arm around* CORNELIA.)

PIERCE: We can find little ways to pass the time.

CORNELIA: Only thirty-six days, more or less, to go.

PIERCE: And more little ways.

(*He kisses her.* MAGGIE *plays a 'time and bells' flourish. Piano comes in, echoing* MAGGIE*'s explorations.*)

CORNELIA: I feel the minutes flying by already.

(*He kisses her again.*)

PIERCE: Promise me you'll stay strong.

CORNELIA: I'll always find strength to keep up with you.

MAGGIE (*singing*): What you are called to do

    You are called to do

    With all of your might.

PIERCE: Each furlong of ocean we leave behind, the horizon calls me all the more to rise and greet it fully.

CORNELIA: And yet, out here, that horizon is always out of reach.

PIERCE: I must seek my proper place, Nelie.

CORNELIA: In Rome it will come clear.

PIERCE: It is as clear to me now as ever. My place is to be a priest.

CORNELIA: My love, a married man cannot be a Catholic priest.

PIERCE: How can I betray my true nature, my highest purpose?

CORNELIA: How could you be a priest and remain a married man?

PIERCE: I will consult those who can advise and direct me.

CORNELIA: Do you mean this?

PIERCE: Yes.

CORNELIA: But what would happen to me and the children?

PIERCE: I'm sure there's a way.

CORNELIA: What kind of way?

PIERCE: As I said, I will seek guidance, as you always encourage me to do.

CORNELIA: Now I wish this voyage would go on for ever.

PIERCE: I promise that when we reach Marseilles I'll find you another nurse for the little ducklings – a French nurse who is not a goose.

CORNELIA: What does the nurse matter now?

PIERCE: Fear not, Nelie, everything will work out for the best.

(PIERCE *goes.*)

CORNELIA: Dear God…

MAGGIE (*singing*): What you are called to do
    You are called to do
    With all of your might.

CORNELIA: Dear God… If we're in your hands… Dear God, are we…? Are we still in your hands?

(*Surge on piano of disordered 'Veni Creator Spiritus'.*)

CORNELIA: Where in the name of heaven are you taking us?

(*Wind blows, sea swells, waves surge.*)

7

ETERNAL CITY

Eleven-year-old IRIS *appears. She is very quiet.*

MAGGIE: How are you doing, honey?

(She goes to hug her. IRIS *shrugs it off.)*

MAGGIE: Is Luke ready?

(IRIS *shakes her head.*)

MAGGIE: Can you nip in and get him?
IRIS: He's not coming.
MAGGIE: What d'you mean?
IRIS: He's gone to his friend's.
MAGGIE: But he knows Saturday is our day when I come up
    to see you both.
IRIS: I told him.
MAGGIE: Didn't Dad tell him?

(IRIS *is silent.*)

MAGGIE: Did Dad make the arrangement on purpose?

(IRIS *is silent again.*)

MAGGIE: OK. We can do something you want then.

(MAGGIE *puts out her hand to* IRIS. IRIS *puts her hands into her pockets.*)

MAGGIE: Don't worry, love. I'll see to it for next time.

(IRIS *follows* MAGGIE *off. Verdi's 'Waltz in F Major' plays on piano.* PIERCE *and* CORNELIA *dance-race each other.*)

PIERCE: Keep up, Nelie!
CORNELIA: Look!
PIERCE: Where?
CORNELIA: Can't you see! The Basilica!
PIERCE: Aha! St Peter's!
CORNELIA: I saw it first!
PIERCE: We're here.

(*Flapping of bird wing.* PIERCE *and* CORNELIA *look up to the sky.*)

CORNELIA: And see those different flocks... Look, turning together.
PIERCE: United as one above the universal Church.
CORNELIA: I must explore each ruin, each arch, cross every single bridge...
PIERCE: Give me your hand, Nelie...
CORNELIA: When will you enquire about priesthood?
PIERCE: For now, give me your hand and together we'll gain entry into the finest palaces.

(CORNELIA *reaches out to* PIERCE. *He takes her hand.*)

PIERCE: Here we are.

CORNELIA: Can you feel the rubble of time beneath your soles? Can you taste the dust of ages, Pierce?

PIERCE: I believe that remarkable experiences might unfold for us here.

CORNELIA: So much to study. So very much to learn.

(MAGGIE *is on the phone.*)

MAGGIE: Didn't fit...? Have you tried them on, Luke...? How are they the wrong kind of boots...? Oh, for AstroTurf? Of course, I know studs are different... No but you have to... I mean, somebody has to let me know... Can you use a pair of Iris's old ones...? They should fit you now... OK, all right... But I have to be told, you see, Luke... told what it is you need...

(*Flapping of bird wing* PIERCE, *prepares to travel again.*)

CORNELIA: Away already?

PIERCE: To undertake pressing business in England.

CORNELIA: How so?

PIERCE: On behalf of Lord Shrewsbury himself.

CORNELIA: How are your enquiries?

PIERCE: They are progressing.

CORNELIA: I urge you to reconsider.

PIERCE: How can you ask this, Nelie?

CORNELIA: How can I not ask?

PIERCE: How can I miss this opportunity to consult the most well-connected theologians of high standing?

CORNELIA: You simply cannot become a priest. No matter how much you desire it. Not while I live.

PIERCE: My, there's an outburst.

CORNELIA: I love you and my darling children. Is this not the most natural thing in the world? Why should I give you up?

PIERCE: We must be guided by what is for the greater good.

(*Flapping of bird wing.*)

PIERCE: Write to me, little one, of what you see whilst I'm away.

CORNELIA: Travel safely.

PIERCE: Oh, Nelie, at least say you'll think of me.

CORNELIA: I will pray for you. That I promise.

(PIERCE *goes, searching for something that equally eludes and compels him. Blue sky. Flapping of bird wing.* MAGGIE *is waiting. She holds two children's backpacks.*)

MAGGIE: Where are you? Where the hell are you?

(CORNELIA *gathers sketchbook and pencils/watercolours.*)

CORNELIA: Persevere with patience. Oh, God help me, how much patience!

(*Church bells ring.* CORNELIA *sits in the park by Santa Sabina church, taking in the view of Rome.*)

CORNELIA (*as she sketches/paints*): *Sette colli de Roma… Celio…
Campidoglio.* Yes, Practise, practise, practise, each attempt
more careful than the last. Is this the way… can this be
my way through, somehow? Practise, practise, practise.

(PETE *faces* MAGGIE.)

MAGGIE: Three hours!

PETE: What's the problem now?

MAGGIE: You knew I had a train to catch. We agreed you'd
be here for me to bring them home in time for tea.

PETE: You said you'd take them for tea.

MAGGIE: My train was two hours ago. I've missed it. They're
hungry and tired. I couldn't contact you. This isn't
clever, it's bloody cruel.

PETE: You said you'd take them somewhere for tea and bring
them home after.

MAGGIE: You know we didn't agree that!

PETE: I'd better go and give them some food, then.

MAGGIE: And why do you make them choose between
speaking with me on the phone or watching TV?

PETE: Your demands are disruptive enough to their routine.

MAGGIE: Your self-serving idea of a routine changes by the
second!

PETE: It's about time you learned to put the children first.

MAGGIE: Here!

(MAGGIE *throws the backpacks at* PETE.)

PETE: And I'm telling them what you just did to their stuff.

(PETE *picks up the backpacks and goes.*)

MAGGIE: Dear God…

CORNELIA: Dear God, please guide me to learn all I must truly learn… How do I… How on earth do I begin to accept what is given, simply as it is given?

(*She falls into the silence, painting.*)

CORNELIA: *Esquilino… Palatino… Quirinale…*

(GWENDALINE *appears: English, nineteen-year-old daughter of Lord Shrewsbury, wife of aristocratic heir Marcantonio Borghese.*)

CORNELIA: *Palatino… Quirinale…*
GWENDALINE: *Viminale…*
CORNELIA: And the seventh hill?
GWENDALINE: You're sitting on it.
CORNELIA: Ah, *Aventino.*
GWENDALINE: How's Merty's fever?
CORNELIA: He was more settled this morning. And Ady slept through last night, thank heavens. Then I received a letter from England.
GWENDALINE: From Pierce?
CORNELIA: He's hugely impressed with your father's great house.
GWENDALINE: I hope you'll one day visit Alton Towers for yourself.
CORNELIA: Perhaps.
GWENDALINE: I have a feeling you'd like England.
CORNELIA: I was not invited this time.

GWENDALINE: Never mind – my sister's to invite you to her party at the palazzo Doria Pamphilj.

CORNELIA: Is the ballroom really golden?

GWENDALINE: *Uno tesoro di Roma.*

CORNELIA: Think of it – little American me among the duchesses and princesses.

GWENDALINE: Bring your best dancing shoes.

CORNELIA: I'll even wear them to the consecration of the new bishop.

GWENDALINE: Pope Gregory may waltz your way. I hear he's to address you in person.

CORNELIA: Then Pierce will be doubly peeved to miss it.

GWENDALINE: I'm sure you'll hold your own.

CORNELIA: He'll have his audience when he returns, to become a priest.

GWENDALINE: Is this decided now for sure?

CORNELIA: I suppose it must be.

GWENDALINE: Why on earth would he give up you, give up his family like this?

(Flapping of bird wing.)

CORNELIA: Perhaps whatever unfolds in our little lives has a greater purpose than we can see down here.

GWENDALINE: I hope so.

CORNELIA: And each time we visit the poor in the shadows of this grand city, Gwendaline, I am reminded to appreciate how very fortunate I am.

(Flapping of bird wing.)

CORNELIA: We must remember to look up to eternal heaven above us… day in, day out… and trust to what our Maker knows that we cannot.

GWENDALINE: You have a searching soul, my dear.

CORNELIA: Dare I live fully by it, I wonder.

(GWENDALINE *kisses* CORNELIA *on the cheek fondly and departs.*)

CORNELIA: Each day I ask how to give up what is most dear. How in the name of God is it done?

(MAGGIE *is on the phone.*)

MAGGIE: Honey, I've found you the perfect new backpack… Yes, I'll bring it next Saturday when I visit… And also the songbook you wanted… What do you mean there's no point…? Are you OK, Iri…? Is there anything else you need? Just let me know… You can always let me know…

(PIERCE *returns from his travels.*)

PIERCE: If only you could see what I have seen these last five months. Such an estate. Such grandeur. What a life.

CORNELIA: Surely your mind has been on other matters too?

PIERCE: Still reading this mind of mine, even from afar?

CORNELIA: The distance seems to make my eyes clearer.

PIERCE: The children have grown more than I expected. I've missed you all so much, my darling.

CORNELIA: Stop.

(PIERCE *opens his arms.* CORNELIA *steps back.*)

CORNELIA: Please. You cannot speak to me like this. Not now you're to give your life to the Church.

PIERCE: My dear...

CORNELIA: Forgive me. I still have too much pride.

PIERCE: My dear, I've studied, discussed, considered a great deal.

CORNELIA: As have I.

PIERCE: I've received the kindest attention from all the first people, cardinals, notable Jesuits...

CORNELIA: I now understand, Pierce, I do. I see that if you are to devote everything to the Kingdom of Heaven, then it follows that because our children and I are also under God's good care, then we too must receive all you give.

PIERCE: The verdict I have received is clear.

CORNELIA: So I have decided to serve you in your sacred work, and promise to try as best I can to be the better part of myself.

PIERCE: The Cardinal Vicar thinks that the example of my conversion will have more impact less as a priest than as a married man.

CORNELIA: What do you say?

PIERCE: Not as a priest, Nelie.

CORNELIA: But what of your true vocation?

PIERCE: I've been instructed to be a good layman instead.

CORNELIA: Is this really the view of the Church?

PIERCE: I endeavour to be useful in whatever way is counselled.

CORNELIA: But we are to meet Pope Gregory.

PIERCE: And the occasion will not be to separate us but to affirm our lives together, our lives and our faith.

CORNELIA: Are you sure?

(PIERCE *holds out his hand to her.*)

PIERCE: Will you, Mrs Connelly?

CORNELIA: Is your mind at rest at last?

PIERCE: Do me the honour of dancing?

('Musetta's Waltz' plays on the piano. Golden light stirs. The ballroom of the Palazzo Doria Pamphilj.)

CORNELIA: So here we are.

PIERCE: In the golden ballroom…

CORNELIA: …of the Palazzo Doria Pamphilj.

PIERCE: Let your yes be…

(*She takes his hand.*)

CORNELIA: Yes.

PIERCE: Yes!

(*He swoops her into a swirl and they dance in each other's arms.* MAGGIE *makes a call on her phone and waits for it to be answered.* 'Musetta's Waltz' *swirls. Golden light fills the space. A sublime moment.*)

PIERCE: Look at us.

CORNELIA: Yes, we are here.

PIERCE: Indeed, we are!

CORNELIA: In the most glorious... miraculous... ballroom
of the grandest grand tour...

PIERCE: All Europe is now ours to explore.

CORNELIA: This never-ever-ending moment!

PIERCE: How much faster further shall we go?

CORNELIA: Ah, the light-fantastic toe!

(They spin together. MAGGIE paces as she repeatedly makes calls, none of which get any response. CORNELIA emerges from the spin holding a baby bundle in her arms.)

CORNELIA: Welcome, my new little duckling.

PIERCE: Let's give him my father's name... and my brother's, too.

CORNELIA: Well, then... Here you are... John Baptist...
Henry... Maria... Louis... Connelly. Hello, dear John
Henry.

(Bell rings, calling them over the ocean.)

PIERCE: Our ship leaves in three days.

CORNELIA: Three days? But the rest of Europe calls. Paris
calls.

PIERCE: Nelie, our finances.

CORNELIA: We can manage, surely?

PIERCE: And our mission calls.

CORNELIA: Our mission. Of course.

PIERCE: Back home.

(MAGGIE puts away her phone.)

MAGGIE: Persevere, be patient, be dogged... As a matter of damn principle, you had better be so unshakeably patient, so incredibly bloody persistent... so utterly resolutely fiercely determined...

(PETE *appears, holding a large envelope.*)

PETE: Be advised, any further correspondence from you to either Iris or Luke will not be returned, as I'm taking the trouble to do this time.

(PETE *empties the envelope and masses of postcards tumble to the ground.*)

PETE: In future it will be destroyed.

MAGGIE: And how am I to keep in touch with them during the week?

PETE: Stick to your appointed times if you must insist on putting them through seeing you.

MAGGIE: I miss them. And they have every right...

PETE: You have no right to miss them. No right at all. And it only makes them upset.

(PETE *leaves.*)

8

LITTLE LAMB

'Little Maggie' music reprise. PIERCE *leads* CORNELIA, *little* JOHN HENRY, ADY *and* MERTY *onwards.*

CORNELIA: My, it's humid.

PIERCE: Keep up, everyone!

MERTY/ADY: Whoooo!

PIERCE: Down the mighty Mississippi. On to Louisiana.

CORNELIA: See, children! See the big swamp. See the plantation.

MERTY: Are we there now?

CORNELIA: Oh, and another big swamp.

ADY: Does anyone else live here?

CORNELIA: Is there a bakery, at least, in Grand Coteau?

PIERCE: I gather so. And most importantly, a post office.

ADY: When are we there?

PIERCE: Aha. Look.

CORNELIA: You mean that little house?

PIERCE: Gracemere, yes. See?

CORNELIA/CHILDREN: We see.

(Music stops. A blustery day on the beach. Wind. Waves. MIKE *and* MAGGIE *look to the horizon.)*

MAGGIE: He can't be allowed to get away with this. I've kept a record of every single incident. It's abusive behaviour.

MIKE: It's a question of proof, love.

MAGGIE: I can get evidence.

MIKE: And who are your witnesses?

MAGGIE: Iris and Luke can confirm what he does… The latest is docking their pocket money if they mention me.

MIKE: You want to put them through testifying against their own father? They're living with him.

MAGGIE: That's exactly the point. So he loses custody and I can look after them properly.

MIKE: It'll cost you in every way. And them more.

(*Waves. Wind.*)

MAGGIE: Don't you want them to live with us?

MIKE: The kind of arrangement we have with my kids… holidays, weekends… Of course I'm up for that…

MAGGIE: But if I could get full custody…

MIKE: The law is highly unlikely to grant it.

MAGGIE: Well, it bloody well ought to!

(*A baby screams.* CORNELIA *coughs and carries another baby bundle.*)

PIERCE: No better today?

CORNELIA: Only a little colic.

(CORNELIA *coughs.*)

PIERCE: What about you?

CORNELIA: Just a silly cough.

PIERCE: Oughtn't you rest?

CORNELIA: I rest when I can.

(*The baby screams. She coughs again.*)

CORNELIA: I'd like to call her Mary Magdalen.

PIERCE: After she who lived repentant?

CORNELIA: And served our Lord faithfully. He loved her very much.

PIERCE: Then let this one be so loved.

(CORNELIA *coughs.*)

CORNELIA: I hope and pray that she will be.

(*Violin/*MERTY *plays 'Mary Had A Little Lamb'.* ADELINE *claps along. Two-year-old* JOHN HENRY *copies the bigger children. Dog barks.*)

CORNELIA: Well done, Merty. Now, Ady.

ADY (*singing*): Mary had a little lamb
    Little lamb, little lamb
    Mary had a little lamb
    Its fleece was white as snow.

All (*singing*): And everywhere that Mary went
    Mary went, Mary went
    Everywhere that Mary went
    The lamb was sure to go.

(CORNELIA *coughs.* PIERCE *withdraws, tries to write a letter.*)

CORNELIA (*singing quietly*): It followed her to school one day…
MERTY/ADY (*singing*): School one day, school one day…
JOHN HENRY: Ooh on day.
MERTY/ADY/CORNELIA (*singing*): It made the children
laugh and play
To see a lamb at school.

(PIERCE *coughs loudly in a request for quiet.* ADY *approaches*
PIERCE.)

ADY: Who are you writing to, Papa?
PIERCE: Do you remember Lord Shrewsbury? From when
you were little in Rome?
ADY: What are you writing to the Lord?
PIERCE: To tell him our news about your new sister.
ADY: Is he important?
PIERCE: Very. So I'm also letting him know about all the pupils
my blessed little wife, your mama, has for piano and sing-
ing at the Sacred Heart Convent. And how I'm a master
and treated like a reverend père at the Jesuit College.
ADY: Pere means Papa.
PIERCE: Here it's the holy kind of a father.
ADY: Can I help you post the letter?
PIERCE: Better post it tomorrow morning straight away.
ADY: Crack of dawn.
PIERCE: Good idea. And when his reply comes, it will bring
some excitement, don't you think?
ADY: Even more than baby Mary arriving?
PIERCE: Now Ady, every day I bless the great star of happi-
ness for the gift of one of the loveliest families, especially
the very best daughters, on earth.

(CORNELIA *coughs, holding, rocking her swaddled, bundled, baby daughter.* MERTY *plays and sings, calling* ADY *to join him.*)

MERTY (*singing*): Why does the lamb love Mary so?
    Love Mary so, love Mary so;
    Why does the lamb love Mary so?
    The eager children cry.
ADY (*singing*): Why, Mary loves the lamb, you know,
    Lamb you know, lamb you know;
    Why, Mary loves the lamb, you know,
    The teacher did reply!

(*Wind. Waves.*)

MAGGIE: What more can I possibly do?
MIKE: God knows.
MAGGIE: I should have brought them… when I left… taken
    them with me. Why did I leave them behind?

(*Dog barks.*)

JOHN HENRY: Mama!
CORNELIA: What's that all over you, John Henry!
ADY: It's coal from the scuttle.
CORNELIA: What a messy pup.
JOHN HENRY: Mary, Mary ickle lamp, ickle lamp!
ADY: Not a lamp, Johnny, a lamb, a lamb.
JOHN HENRY: A lamp a lamp a lamp!
MERTY: Ha ha! Mary had a little lamp!
PIERCE: And I'm sure a very bright lamp it was too!
MERTY: Little lamp, little lamp!

PIERCE: And now it's time…

ADY/MERTY: Mary had a little lamp, little lamp, little lamp!

PIERCE: Time to turn out the light!

(*Piano plays variation of 'Mary Had a Little Lamb'.* CORNELIA *loosens hold of the swaddling for baby* MARY, *lets it unravel. Waves. Wind.*)

MAGGIE: What more could I have done?

CORNELIA (*singing/coughing*): Mary had a little lamp, little lamp…

…followed it about…

Cool breeze blew… Cool… breeze… blew…

And blew… the lamp right… (Speaks) out.

(CORNELIA *carefully folds the swaddling into a tight pile.* ADY *goes to* PIERCE. *He holds her tight.* JOHN HENRY *hovers at* CORNELIA's *legs.* MERTY *hovers between* CORNELIA *and* PIERCE. CORNELIA *coughs. She lays down the blanket.*)

PIERCE: Rest in peace, little Mary.

ADY/MERTY: Rest in peace.

CORNELIA: How much more could I have done?

(CORNELIA *withdraws into herself, away from the rest of her family. She coughs.*)

MAGGIE: How can I let him turn me into a punishment for my own children?

PIERCE: Come, Nelie, give me your hand.

(MIKE *reaches out to* MAGGIE. *She withdraws into herself. He nods and leaves.* CORNELIA *stands alone and coughs.*)

PIERCE: My dear, please take care of yourself. I need… we all need you better.

CORNELIA: Forgive me.

PIERCE: I know you must bear a heavy conscience.

CORNELIA: For being so unwell.

PIERCE: You must get well, Nelie.

CORNELIA: I shall make a retreat with the nuns.

PIERCE: How long will you be away?

MAGGIE: There must be another way.

CORNELIA: We must learn to leave ourselves, maintain a rule of life and daily practice, morning meditation.

MAGGIE: What can I do?

(*'Mary Had a Little Lamb' reprise.*)

9

SUGAR SYRUP

Cool, bright sunlight shines and dapples. Birdsong. The children burst into life.

MERTY/ADY/JOHN HENRY: Mama! Mama!

(CORNELIA *opens her arms to her children.*)

CORNELIA: There you are! Come, ducklings.

(*Birdsong.*)

CORNELIA: What could be more beautiful than all this nature around all around and around and around us!

(CORNELIA *waltzes with her children – whirling together in the sunshine. Water drips.* MAGGIE *is in the chapel of the convent at St Leonards. She holds a child's violin case on her lap.*)

MAGGIE: Cornelia?

(*Suddenly light dapples* CORNELIA's *face.*)

MAGGIE: Luke left his violin by the bins. When I dropped him off, I picked it up to take it in. He refused to have it in the house. He told me it's rubbish.

CORNELIA: Oh my God! If such happiness is not to thy greater glory... for the good of my soul... then I pray, take it from me. I surrender entirely. I make the sacrifice.

MAGGIE: Is it me? Am I the one who must change now?

CORNELIA (*in prayer*): Oh my God, trim thy vine...

(MAGGIE *improvises 'Oh My God, Trim Thy Vine', singing heart and soul.*)

MAGGIE (*singing*): Oh my God, trim thy vine...

(PIERCE *appears.*)

PIERCE: Nelie, look! Winter is beginning to end. Can't you see, it's sugarin' season. They're slicing the maple trees, bleeding the sap. Out it flows into the baskets.

MAGGIE (*singing*): ...Cut it to the quick.

CORNELIA (*in prayer*): ...but in Thy great mercy root it not yet up.

PIERCE: Pure and fresh with no colour, no smell, no flavour at all.

CORNELIA (*in prayer*): My God, help me in my great weakness...

PIERCE: We must dig out a fresh pit and stoke the fire.

MAGGIE (*singing*): But in thy great mercy...

PIERCE: On goes our great pot. In pours our clear sap.

CORNELIA (*in prayer*): Please help me.

MAGGIE (*singing*): ...Root it not yet up.

PIERCE: Let the transformation begin.

CORNELIA (*in prayer*): Help me to serve you with new fervour.

PIERCE: Leave it boil, and as it boils, see it thicken and darken. We'll have our fresh sugar syrup for spring.

(*Dog barks.* JOHN HENRY *laughs.*)

MAGGIE (*singing*): Oh my God, trim thy vine
Cut it to the quick
PIERCE: Look how it bubbles. Just a few more logs for the fire.
MAGGIE (*singing*): But in thy great mercy…

(*Dog barks.* JOHN HENRY *plays and laughs. 'Oh My God, Trim Thy Vine' melody plays on piano.*)

MAGGIE: How can I leave my family and try to hang on at the same time? Who am I kidding? What if… to protect them… I must… for my children's sakes… the only way now… for their sakes… so they're not torn in two…

(*Dog barks and barks.* JOHN HENRY *laughs and laughs. Suddenly the music, laughter and barking stop. Silence.*)

CORNELIA: Pierce?
PIERCE: He was playing.
CORNELIA: But how did he fall into the boiling syrup? Did he try to taste it? Didn't anyone see? How did he fall into the boiling syrup? Where were you?
PIERCE: That stupid dog.
CORNELIA: Are you saying it was the dog… Are you saying the dog pushed him?
PIERCE: Maybe he fell.

CORNELIA: What made him fall? What? How? Weren't you there? Was no one there? Did no one see…? How long was he in there…? Is it too late now… Did we get here too late…?

PIERCE: I've put out the fire.

CORNELIA: How do I hold him… when he is so terribly burned…? Careful… careful… Does that hurt, Jonnie…? Sh… Here… Here… just here… on my lap… Here now…

PIERCE: Nelie?

(Piano plays opening chords, echo of 'Oh My God, Trim Thy Vine'.)

CORNELIA: How do I hold him… when he is so terribly burned? Careful… careful… Does that hurt…? Sh… Here… Here… just here… on my lap…

PIERCE: Nelie?

CORNELIA: How can I hold him without it hurting all the more?

PIERCE: If you are to sit in vigil…

CORNELIA: But how can I not hold him?

PIERCE: Then I too shall pray for as long as you sit.

(CORNELIA *sits and cradles the burned child in her arms, like a pietà of the Madonna and dying Christ.*)

CORNELIA: Sh. Sh.

PIERCE (*kneeling*): Let us atone…

CORNELIA: Here, here.

PIERCE: Hour by hour…

CORNELIA: Oh Jesus, your wounds. Oh blessed mother…

PIERCE: Hour upon hour upon hour... hours, hours...

CORNELIA: Mother of Sorrows, do you reveal to me what you bear?

PIERCE: Forty-three hours.

(*Silence.* CORNELIA *lets her arms drop.*)

CORNELIA: John Henry Connelly. Not yet three years old. Fell a victim on Friday and was taken into the temple of the Lord.

MAGGIE: Yes... for my children's sake... I can't have anything to do with them − not for the time being. No. I must let them be.

(MAGGIE *and* CORNELIA *sit side by side. Silence. Stillness.*)

ACT II

10

FLOWERS

Golden light. Piano. Distant, tentative violin. The opening section of 'Bells', MAGGIE's composition, now fully formed, plays. Ten years on, MAGGIE holds two takeaway cups and waits for somebody. Eight months after JOHN HENRY's death, CORNELIA stands before the graves of JOHN HENRY and MARY MAGDALEN. She is pregnant. Birdsong. PIERCE appears, holding a posy of flowers.

PIERCE: Are you well, my dear?

CORNELIA (*touching her belly*): We are both well enough.

PIERCE: And Ady, Merty?

CORNELIA: A few sniffles and moods. Nothing more.

PIERCE: My retreat with the Jesuits has been most instructive.

(PIERCE *gives her the posy of flowers.*)

CORNELIA: Was my own retreat with the nuns only last Christmas? And on my return, who ran to greet me, but John Henry.

(*She looks at the grave.*)

CORNELIA: How can the passing of so few months last a lifetime?

PIERCE: These weeks I've had moment to examine my conscience most deeply.

CORNELIA: Let us hope this new child will be a comfort.

PIERCE: Haven't I loved you as a woman is rarely loved?

CORNELIA: And I you.

PIERCE: Can you still read my mind, hear my heart, Nelie?

CORNELIA: What has your conscience been telling you?

PIERCE: That my foremost duty of love can only ever be in the direct service of God.

CORNELIA: Your foremost duty of love?

PIERCE: Nelie, I have been further reconsidering… and now intend… fully intend to become ordained as a priest.

CORNELIA: What do you say?

PIERCE: Please give your support.

CORNELIA: Reconsider again.

PIERCE: Your consent, your vow is required, alongside mine.

CORNELIA: My vow?

PIERCE: Of celibacy.

CORNELIA: But we are to become mother and father again.

PIERCE: I promise that I shall always fulfil my duties. And, as you say, this new child will be a comfort for you.

CORNELIA: What of a husband's comfort?

PIERCE: Priesthood is a higher calling than marriage.

(*Stunned silence.*)

PIERCE: We can still live alongside one another. As brother and sister.

CORNELIA: Do you honestly wish to end all intimate relations between us?

PIERCE: For the rest of my life.

94

CORNELIA: For my life too?

PIERCE: Please help me to apply for dispensation. Your consent is essential, Nelie.

CORNELIA: And then?

PIERCE: I must return to Rome. With Merty.

CORNELIA: But Pierce, he is only eight.

PIERCE: Don't you wish him to be educated in England as a young gentleman?

CORNELIA: How can we afford it?

PIERCE: Lord Shrewsbury is making arrangements. You need only take care of Adeline and the baby here.

CORNELIA: You and he have it all planned?

PIERCE: He's glad to be of help. I think somehow it eases his own grief.

CORNELIA: Dearest Gwendaline. I miss... I so miss... her kindness... her warm company...

PIERCE: Turn to the sisters of the Sacred Heart here.

CORNELIA: I must continue to teach at the convent.

PIERCE: Where you are much valued.

CORNELIA: In that there is worth and hope, even joy.

PIERCE: Good.

CORNELIA: Please allow Merty to stay in my care too.

PIERCE: This is for his betterment.

CORNELIA: Promise me, whatever you do for him and the others from now on, you will always ask me first.

PIERCE: You are their mother.

CORNELIA: And your wife.

PIERCE: It is a holy thing, Nelie, to make ourselves eunuchs for the sake of the Kingdom of Heaven.

CORNELIA: What am I meant to say?

PIERCE: Please consent.

(CORNELIA *touches her belly.*)

PIERCE: Do you consent?
CORNELIA: Yes.

(PIERCE *leaves.*)

CORNELIA: No.

(*'Bells' plays on piano.*)

CORNELIA: No.

(IRIS, *in her early twenties, appears. She holds a bunch of flowers.*)

MAGGIE: Iris?
IRIS: Mum?

(MAGGIE *is overcome with emotion. She tries to contain herself.*)

MAGGIE: Hello.
IRIS: Hi.
MAGGIE: I got you a coffee.
IRIS: Oh… thanks… but…
MAGGIE: Don't you drink coffee?
IRIS: Not really…
MAGGIE: I shouldn't have presumed… Sorry…
IRIS: Oh, I can… just this once… I mean, I don't mind the taste…
MAGGIE: Don't worry…

(IRIS *offers the flowers.*)

IRIS: Coffee for flowers?

(IRIS *gives the flowers.* MAGGIE *gives the coffee.*)

MAGGIE: Thank you.
IRIS: Thank you.

(*As they swap, they move closer and then they hug.*)

MAGGIE: Careful… It'll spill.

(*They continue to hug.* CORNELIA *places the flowers from* PIERCE *on the children's graves.*)

11

SACRIFICE

Wind blows. Ocean swells. Up on deck, PIERCE *takes in the air and reads over a sermon he has written.*

PIERCE: Sacrifices are required to live a holy life.

(*In the distance a baby cries.*)

PIERCE: But for those devoted and courageous enough to aspire to ascend the ladder, all difficulties are but glorious rewards.

(*Baby cries.*)

PIERCE: For they shall be foremost in the ranks.

(CORNELIA *is rocking her newborn baby son.*)

PIERCE: Some throw off their wealth and surrender into the lap of poverty. Many live among the humble and persecuted.
CORNELIA: Oh, Pierce, do you realise the trials of priesthood?
PIERCE: Others leave their newborn babes in their cradles.
CORNELIA: You can still escape all such difficulties…

(*Baby cries.*)

PIERCE: And some offer a last kiss to a dear wife.

CORNELIA: My arms remain open, dear love…

PIERCE: Then flee from her warm embrace to accompany
the Lamb wherever he might go. For ever.

CORNELIA: Come home. Let us be a family again.

PIERCE: As I strap on my pilgrim sandals afresh, I seek what
I find nowhere else.

(*Baby cries.*)

CORNELIA: What a mighty pair of lungs you have, little
Pierce Francis Connelly.

PIERCE: O beauty so ancient and yet so new, I find all in
thee, holy Church of Rome.

CORNELIA: Sh, Frank, Sh.

(*Baby cries fade. Wind blows. Waves crash upon the shore.* MAGGIE
and IRIS *sit side by side looking out on to the horizon.*)

MAGGIE: And Luke, was he with you that day at Alton
Towers?

IRIS: He was on a ride – didn't see Mike and his sons.

MAGGIE: What are the chances of you bumping into them
like that?

IRIS: It was good it was me they saw, not him.

MAGGIE: Have you told Luke about us being in touch?

IRIS: God, no. He'd tell dad straight away. Nightmare.

MAGGIE: Mightn't it be better for your dad to know?

IRIS: I haven't even told him about dropping law yet.

MAGGIE: Shall I write to him?

IRIS: It's not worth it. But thanks. And thanks for offering to cover my fees.

MAGGIE: I'm in a position to help now.

IRIS: Because of your piano method?

MAGGIE: I'm fortunate it's hit a chord.

IRIS: Have you devised a method for flute too?

MAGGIE: You still have that?

IRIS: Somewhere.

MAGGIE: Would you like to visit the new centre? I could show you round. Hear the choir… or quartet, perhaps…?

IRIS: I have a confession to make.

MAGGIE: Oh?

IRIS: Couple of years ago… I was coming out of some show… you know, and people hand you flyers for concerts… and the picture weirdly leaped out… of a virgin and child… like a modern sculpture… her arms wide open… Then even more weirdly I saw your name… Didn't tell anyone… Went on my own… to a performance of 'Bells'… It wasn't anything I could have expected… kind of soulful and strange and uplifting… quite sad, too.

(*Silence. Shared.*)

IRIS: I wondered if I'd see you there, but I couldn't.

MAGGIE: I wish I'd known.

IRIS: Nearly wrote after the concert… I don't know… Wasn't sure how… Do you compose much?

MAGGIE: Beavering away on my own for years… 'Bells' was a big step… getting a full piece out… Oh Iri, I'm so glad you heard it.

IRIS: Do you actually go to church?

MAGGIE: I prefer churches when there's no one else in them.

IRIS: Do you pray?

MAGGIE: In my own way.

IRIS: How does praying make any difference?

MAGGIE: It can help, apart from anything else, to still the voices in your head... you know, rabbiting on, blaming, anxious, guilty...

IRIS: Doesn't it make you feel even more guilty?

MAGGIE: Maybe at first... But if you stay with whatever comes up instead of pushing it away, let it pass through then surrender it to... I guess you could call it an Eternal Presence...

IRIS: Like God?

MAGGIE: For me it's more like a Mother presence... simply there, holding... accepting... allowing you to find a place beyond it all... silent... spacious... Does this make any sense?

IRIS: Are you saying you have more like a spiritual experience than being religious?

MAGGIE: Well... you know, when you're out in Nature... like by the sea here... you sense that you're not just 'in' the elements... or even part of the elements... you *are* the elements... and able to notice that you are at the same time.

IRIS: Is 'Bells' to do with this?

MAGGIE: I guess all my music... and teaching... is in some way. 'Bells'... you see... I wrote at first from the perspective of hearing bells ringing... and then being the one ringing the bells... and then becoming like the bell itself as it's ringing... and then being the ringing that comes through the bell... pure ringing... whatever that might be...

IRIS: The woman sitting next to me said something like that.

MAGGIE: Oh?

IRIS: She went on your courses… And I told her, 'My mother's Maggie Byrne.' She had no idea you had a daughter.

MAGGIE: Why should she know?

IRIS: You wouldn't have created so much, done this well if we'd been with you, would you?

MAGGIE: Not with your father, no.

IRIS: I mean if you'd had custody of us.

MAGGIE: I hope I might.

IRIS: But how much could you have been around?

MAGGIE: I saw other women manage.

IRIS: Can you really have it both ways?

MAGGIE: Hey, how about I take you out for a birthday dinner next month?

IRIS: You remember?

MAGGIE: Of course. Always. I sent a card and a gift… to each of you. Every year.

IRIS: You did?

MAGGIE: I hoped something might get through at least once.

IRIS: Never.

MAGGIE: Nothing?

IRIS: No. Nothing at all.

12

MATER ADMIRABILIS

'Panis Angelicus' plays. CORNELIA *cradles baby* FRANK *in one arm, holding out her other hand for* ADY.

CORNELIA: Up we climb to the very top of the steps.

(CORNELIA, ADY *and* FRANK *reach the top of the Spanish Steps in the heart of Rome and arrive before a great medieval convent door.* PIERCE *appears to greet them.*)

PIERCE: Here you are.
CORNELIA: Here we are.
PIERCE: All of us again in Rome.
CORNELIA: Not all, Pierce.
PIERCE: Merty is doing well in England.
ADY: Papa!
PIERCE: Dear Ady.

(*They hug tight.*)

PIERCE: So this is little Frank. He seems contented enough.
CORNELIA: He's exhausted from the journey.

(PIERCE *kisses the baby's head.*)

CORNELIA: How long are we are to stay here at Trinità dei Monti?

PIERCE: The Sisters of the Sacred Heart will accommodate you for the entire duration of my training.

CORNELIA: But this will be years.

ADY: Are we going to live in the convent, Papa?

CORNELIA: Might we not move on to some dwelling of our own?

PIERCE: The Church insists.

(*A nun approaches, carrying a Bible.*)

CORNELIA: Do I have full assurance in making this vow that I'm not bound to monastic life?

PIERCE: The vow does not make you a nun, Nelie, only a postulant in training.

CORNELIA: And as such I can continue to take care of my children?

PIERCE: And I have special privileges to visit you all here, too.

(CORNELIA *takes the Bible and carefully gives baby* FRANK *to the nun.*)

CORNELIA: Ady, go with the sisters now. I'll be with you soon.

(*The nun leaves with* FRANK *and* ADY. *A bell rings.* CORNELIA *steps forward, places her hand carefully upon the Bible. A solemn moment.*)

CORNELIA: So, of my own free will... 'Oh God almighty and eternal. I, Cornelia, lawful wife of Pierce Connelly, trusting in your goodness and mercy, desiring to serve you more perfectly, with the consent of my husband who prepares to receive holy orders... do make a vow of perpetual chastity.' Please grant me the grace to accomplish it.

(*A bell rings.* MAGGIE *appears with a cake, bowl of icing and piping bag.* MIKE *holds out candles and holders.*)

MIKE: One candle for each year?

MAGGIE: Of course.

MIKE: At last Iris can blow them out for herself.

MAGGIE: I wish I'd taken photos of each previous year's cake I made, to show her.

MIKE: Nah.

MAGGIE: It's the thought, not the craft, you know.

MIKE: Still, not your best work, love.

MAGGIE: I bet her father didn't bake or decorate a single cake for either of them.

MIKE: Let's hope this one tastes better than it looks.

MAGGIE: You wait.

(MAGGIE *shoos* MIKE *away and starts to ice/decorate this birthday cake. She isn't at all skilled. Time passes. Bells ring.* CORNELIA *dons an apron, sits with paint pots, palette, brush. She mixes a colour.* ADY *appears. She is around nine or ten, and carries a slate and chalk.*)

ADY: I've attended to my studies, Mama.

CORNELIA: Well done, Ady. You must read aloud the next chapter to me tomorrow morning before I give my English lesson.

ADY: Now may I make my own drawing from the fresco?

CORNELIA: Come and look carefully.

(ADY *sits beside* CORNELIA *and gazes at the wall in front of them as she starts to draw.* MAGGIE *surreptitiously licks her fingers.*)

CORNELIA: And what name does Our Lady have here?

ADY: Queen of Heaven.

CORNELIA: Pauline has at last finished scrubbing and preparing the wall, then making the outline. See.

ADY: Is Pauline going to become a sister one day?

CORNELIA: First she must serve her time in preparation as a postulant.

ADY: I'm definitely going to be a sister.

CORNELIA: How can you be so sure?

ADY: Papa is sure that he wants to be a holy father, isn't he?

CORNELIA: Remember, Ady, we must follow not our own wish but God's.

ADY: Mother Josephine says that I have promise.

CORNELIA: You also have promise as an artist. It takes a steady hand and keen eye to make a star so well-proportioned.

(ADY *glows with pride.* MAGGIE *starts to pipe stars and 'HAPPY BIRTHDAY IRIS' on to the cake.*)

CORNELIA: Do you know why there are twelve stars?

ADY: I think I've forgotten.

CORNELIA: In the book of Revelation we are told, '…A great portent appeared in heaven, a woman clothed with the sun, the moon beneath her feet, and on her head a crown of twelve stars.' Only Pauline seems to have left out the moon.

ADY: Even though there is no moon, may I draw it anyhow?

CORNELIA: There's no one here to stop you, is there? And as you do, I must add to Our Lady's sleeve. That pink is far too pale.

ADY: Is that supposed to be a book inside the basket?

CORNELIA: That's the oddest-shaped book I've ever seen.

ADY: Mother Josephine doesn't think Pauline is very capable as an artist, does she?

CORNELIA: We will not spread tittle-tattle, Ady.

ADY: Sorry, Mama.

CORNELIA: Still, is that meant to be a spindle? Looks more like an old broom to me.

(ADY *giggles.*)

CORNELIA: I suspect that Mother Josephine will wince at these colours, but more brightness will do no harm...

(ADY *draws.* CORNELIA *continues to mix the paint.* MAGGIE *concentrates keenly on her wonky piping.*)

CORNELIA: We shall with a little artistry transform this imperfect creature into a... Mother Most Admirable... Mater Admirabilis.

(*The palette tips, splattering paint.*)

CORNELIA: Whoops!

(MAGGIE *smudges badly.*)

MAGGIE: Damn!

(ADY *and* CORNELIA *stare at the mess, then burst into uncontrollable laughter.*)

CORNELIA: What a messy pup.
ADY: Better get you cleaned up.
CORNELIA: And you. Look at your hands, chalky.

(*Bell rings.*)

CORNELIA: And now, we must remember to be on our…?
ADY: Best behaviour.

(CORNELIA *and* ADY *pack up and leave. Making the best of it,* MAGGIE *adds candle holders and candles to the iced cake. Another bell rings.* PIERCE *appears, takes in the view of Rome.* CORNELIA, *now without apron, cleaned up, appears. She winds a flower or two to complete a pretty wreath.*)

PIERCE: You really do have a wonderful view of the city, as if you could leap anywhere in a single bound.
CORNELIA: If only we could.
PIERCE: You will make your peace with these circumstances, I hope, when you fully enter the order.
CORNELIA: This is not yet decided – not at all.
PIERCE: What else will you do once I'm ordained?
CORNELIA: Did you manage to see Frank this morning?
PIERCE: We took a stroll around the garden. He showed me how to spin very fast and make himself so dizzy he falls over.
CORNELIA: Oh, Pierce, I've been encouraging him to slow himself down. He made himself sick yesterday.
PIERCE: I think he's developing a ruddy complexion – very English.

CORNELIA: Merty seems to be happy enough there.

(CORNELIA *takes a letter out of her sleeve and hands it to* PIERCE.)

PIERCE: I shall see him before long.
CORNELIA: Are you to visit his Lordship?
PIERCE: I'm to join his household as chaplain.
CORNELIA: I see.
PIERCE: And don't you agree it's time the younger ones received
the same quality of education as their elder brother?
CORNELIA: Are you planning to take them to England too?
PIERCE: Where else?

(*Silence.*)

PIERCE: I'm sorry to have missed Ady today.
CORNELIA: Will you be present at her first communion?
PIERCE: I'm glad to say it will be my first communion too,
as priest.
CORNELIA: There's a thing – to be Father in both senses.

(*Bells ring.* MAGGIE *adds final touches to the cake. 'Panis Angelicus'
plays on piano.* ADY *appears.* CORNELIA *places the wreath of flowers
upon her head.* PIERCE *dons his priestly robes.* MAGGIE *holds up the
birthday cake.* PIERCE *turns to* ADY *and addresses his homily directly
to her.*)

PIERCE: Remember this day, for here we all come together
and are fully nourished around the table of the Lord.
ADY (*singing*): *Panis angelicus*
Fit panis hominum;

Dat panis cælicus
Figuris terminum:
O res mirabilis!
Manducat Dominum
Pauper, Pauper
Servus et humilis;
Pauper, Pauper
Servus et humilis

(Bread of angels
becomes the bread of mortals;
Bread of heaven
ends all symbols;
Oh, miraculous thing!
The body of the Lord will nourish
Even the poorest, poor
humble servant;
Poor, poor
humble servant)

PIERCE: Celebrate the anniversary each year, for Jesus is in the Eucharist to be received in love. Wherever there is a priest, Jesus is present, for the priest's mission in Holy Mass is to transform the bread and wine into the body and blood of the Lord.

(PIERCE *puts his hand on* ADY*'s head, blessing her.*)

PIERCE: Celebrate here, and in heaven too. Be innocent. For in you lies the mystery held in every child's soul, created directly by God our Father who provides for us all.

(*Silence falls.*)

PIERCE: 'Let the children come to me! Do not hinder them!'

13

VOCATION

Night-time. Darkness. CORNELIA *carries a candle and paces the convent cloisters. Water drips.* MAGGIE *sits in the chapel at St Leonards.*

CORNELIA: Oh, Blessed Lady, how can I bear any longer to be shut within these Sacred Heart walls?

MAGGIE: If only I'd kept my mouth shut...

CORNELIA: If only I were once more dancing in the golden ballroom in my husband's arms.

MAGGIE: But why should I bite my tongue?

CORNELIA: If only all my children were still sleeping soundly to wake in the morning at home.

MAGGIE: Riding a bicycle with no helmet is plain reckless. Why can't I look out for her without getting an earful in return?

CORNELIA: Must my little ones leave me for ever locked in this place?

MAGGIE: Must my daughter for ever mistrust and resent me?

CORNELIA: Am I to be lost to the world?

MAGGIE: All those damn lost years.

CORNELIA: Is this the meaning of desolation?

MAGGIE: How do I reach out... without seeming needy or controlling... without messing it up... making her pull away...?

CORNELIA: What is my place?

MAGGIE: Why couldn't we have been together when she needed me most?

CORNELIA: Help me to reconcile my duties as wife and mother and Christian.

MAGGIE: Face it, some things can never be reconciled.

(MAGGIE *puts her head in her hands.* CORNELIA *puts her hand to her heart.*)

CORNELIA: Do you call to me, Blessed Mother?

(*Simple notes echo 'Veni Creator Spiritus'.*)

CORNELIA: Is this you I sense, here now, in this still breaking heart?

(CORNELIA *listens, as* MAGGIE *listens.*)

MAGGIE: All these years... devoted to so many... nurturing their creativity and learning...

CORNELIA: To endure my earthly fate I must surrender to the greater fate God prescribes.

MAGGIE: Enabling... encouraging... raising spirits... developing skills... opening to new horizons...

CORNELIA: For those who teach others shall shine as stars in heaven.

MAGGIE: And those who teach others shall shine as stars in heaven.

CORNELIA: I must go out beyond these cloisters.

MAGGIE: I know... I get it... I had to get beyond... because my heart was breaking open... bursting with possibilities...

CORNELIA: I open myself utterly to the needs of the day, of the poor, of all children in the wide world.

MAGGIE: But how does tending all those others make up for losing my own?

(*A bell rings.*)

CORNELIA: When I step through muddy streets, let me love God with my feet. When I toil, love Him with my hands. When I teach the children, let me love most with His little ones.

MAGGIE: I know she isn't little any more…

CORNELIA: If, O God, you are pleased to place me in religious life…

MAGGIE: So why do I feel like I still keep letting go of her hand…

CORNELIA: Let me offer myself to found and head a new congregation.

MAGGIE: Why couldn't my lesson have been to deal with supporting them both and all the rest too?

CORNELIA: And let this order bear the name of the Holy Child Jesus. Its mission must be to undertake active duties of spiritual mercy.

MAGGIE: Serving the needs of others is an honour, a joy… BUT…

CORNELIA: And I shall serve as a Reverend Mother. Mother to many.

MAGGIE: Where's my place as my children's mother now?

CORNELIA: Show me my place now. Out there. Where?

14

NEW ORDER

MERTY, *now fourteen years old, plays 'The Derby Ram' on violin.* ADY, *now eleven, accompanies on flute.* FRANK, *five years old, watches and draws.* PIERCE *and* CORNELIA *also watch.* MAGGIE *is searching for something.*

MAGGIE: It's been stored safely away for long enough.
MERTY (*singing*): As I went out to Derby, upon a market day,
  I spied the biggest ram, sir, that ever was fed on hay.
  And indeed, sir, 'tis true, sir, I never was given to lie,
  And if you've been to Derby, sir,
  You'd have seen him as well as I.

  The horns upon his head, sir, held a regiment of men,
  And the tongue that was in his head, sir, held a regiment
  of men...

(ADY *joins in with the chorus.*)

MERTY/ADY (*singing*): And indeed, sir, 'tis true, sir, I never
  was given to lie,
  And if you've been to Derby, sir,
  You'd have seen him as well as I.
MERTY: The tail was fifty yards, sir, as near as I can tell,
  And it was sent to Rome, sir, to ring St Peter's bell...

(PIERCE *interrupts the song.*)

PIERCE: I thought you were going to play the Handel for us.

MERTY: I wanted to give Mama a surprise.

CORNELIA: Thank you, Merty. Now I know to seek out the
market when I arrive in Derby.

MERTY: It's not real... the ram... I don't think it ever truly
existed... It's meant to be a joke... an English joke.

CORNELIA: Are you drawing the ram, Frank?

FRANK: I'm drawing the elephant.

CORNELIA: Do you mean the marble figure in the hallway?

(FRANK *shows her his picture.*)

CORNELIA: Have you done this from memory?

PIERCE: My, that's a very tall elephant.

CORNELIA: Do you want to go look at the figure again while
you draw?

(FRANK *nods and runs off with his picture and pencil.*)

ADY: Mama, may I go and play in the garden?

CORNELIA: See if the gardener will help you pick some
herbs.

(ADY *runs off.*)

PIERCE: Come, Merty. Let's hear you do Handel some
justice.

MERTY: I need to practise it again first, Papa.

PIERCE: You do that.

(MERTY *withdraws and practises 'Sonata in E Major' by Handel.*
MAGGIE *finds a child-sized violin case.*)

CORNELIA: How is Lord Shrewsbury?

PIERCE: He has another chaplain with us at Alton Towers.

CORNELIA: So, you are the second chaplain?

PIERCE: For the time being, it seems.

CORNELIA: And is your advice sought?

PIERCE: Less than I hoped.

CORNELIA: It is still a good position, is it not?

PIERCE: I understand that Bishop Wiseman has found you
an unexpectedly large convent.

CORNELIA: Well, this is the first order of nuns to be founded
on English soil.

PIERCE: I know.

CORNELIA: I hear there is much need in Derby of our new
school, too.

PIERCE: I hope that you'll ensure the suitability of conditions
at this school of yours for Ady and Frank.

CORNELIA: The Bishop has only yesterday given instructions that it is essential for me to be entirely devoted to
the holy work.

PIERCE: Has he indeed?

CORNELIA: So they must settle at schools elsewhere.

(CORNELIA *turns her attention to* MERTY*'s playing.* PIERCE
bursts into applause before MERTY *finishes.* MERTY *stops playing, bows dutifully, places his violin to one side, quietly leaves.*
MAGGIE *opens the violin case. She takes out the child's violin and
tries to tune it.*)

PIERCE: Does the Bishop not understand our particular situation?

CORNELIA: Our situation… as husband and wife… our continued involvement… is considered… most abnormal.

PIERCE: I shall go and see the Bishop personally.

CORNELIA: Please do not.

PIERCE: Have you already agreed to this?

CORNELIA: I have it all in hand, Pierce. I am persuaded that it is most sensible for the time being to let them follow the same path as Merty. It has suited him well enough. And founding this new order will take all my attention as I prepare fully to take my vows.

PIERCE: Vows?

CORNELIA: Then, once the convent and school have been established, I may be allowed to make accommodation – certainly for Ady… and I hope Merty may visit… and we shall see what is best for Frank.

PIERCE: Vows, Nelie?

CORNELIA: I have only so far taken the first of three.

PIERCE: But our children need you.

CORNELIA: This is merely for the time being.

PIERCE: What about your duty as a mother?

CORNELIA: As a priest, you know full well that I owe total obedience to the Bishop.

PIERCE: There can be no possibility of your taking full vows. I will not allow this.

CORNELIA: Please let's make the most of these precious days we have together, all of us here now.

PIERCE: Are you truly prepared to give up the children?

CORNELIA: Be assured, I shall keep my eye on them as much as ever.

PIERCE: Do not underestimate the demands of convent life, Nelie.

CORNELIA: Fear not, Pierce, everything will work out for the best.

(PIERCE *departs.* MAGGIE *plucks a few notes on the child's violin – minor echoes of 'The Derby Ram'. Piano plays the end of the chorus.* CORNELIA *picks up the earthy energy of the folk song with lively anticipation as she dons her habit, rising in stature for her new role as Reverend Mother.*)

15

SIX HOURS

IRIS *appears wearing a bike helmet; she unfastens then removes it.*
MAGGIE *meets her.*

MAGGIE: Is that helmet new?
IRIS: Amir bought it for me.

(MAGGIE *nods quietly.*)

MAGGIE: How's it going with him?
IRIS: Yeah good. We've been having a homey stint. He's baking bread and I've made preserves. How many jars of gooseberry jam would you like?

(*At the convent and school in Derby.* EMILY, *a young nun, wearing the same habit as* CORNELIA, *leaps for high ground and screams.*)

CORNELIA: Shoo! Shoo!
EMILY: Where is it? Where is it now?
CORNELIA: It's gone. I think, Sister Emily, that you are safe.

(EMILY *sheepishly climbs down.*)

EMILY: Forgive me, Mother Cornelia.

CORNELIA: We shall make a new assault on them this week. And remember, it is important that we encourage the young ladies to retain their composure and realise the ineffectiveness of screaming at rats.

EMILY: Yes of course, Mother Cornelia.

CORNELIA: The things we must teach.

EMILY: The things we must learn.

CORNELIA: Deeds not words. Please be their guide.

EMILY: I shall pray for strength.

CORNELIA: Think of Frank – he'd probably want to be friends with one and make it into a pet.

EMILY: Ugh.

CORNELIA: Look again, look again, through the eyes of the child.

EMILY: Is he well?

CORNELIA: Happy as happy, I hear. And Ady writes that she is feeling stronger after her bout of chicken pox.

EMILY: They must be missing you.

CORNELIA: And I them. Still, I pray for them every day. And at least we may correspond regularly… Although Merty has not written for a while… I must send him another reminder…

(CORNELIA *takes a little package out of her pocket.*)

CORNELIA: Now, look what has been donated by the dairy…

EMILY: Butter!

CORNELIA: So let's invite the parish priest to our charity tea... find him an extra slice of bread... And if we pray for a dash of honey too... well, it might not be the rent he's after... but we can hope that he'll not glare at us quite so much whenever we pass him by...

EMILY: When was the last time you tasted honey... or even jam?

CORNELIA: When was the last time I could feel all my toes?

EMILY: Let me warm you up a little.

(EMILY *plays Verdi's 'Waltz In F Major' on the piano.* CORNELIA *starts to pace out a waltz.*)

CORNELIA: Ah... Right foot back on One... Left foot to the side on Two... Rise and fall... Rise and fall... We must encourage the girls to dance more... and paint... and sing... and make plays... All the behaviour that sustains a bright spirit... Rise and fall... Rise and fall...

EMILY: Is this allowed?

CORNELIA: Why ever not?

EMILY: Won't the Bishop regard waltzing as rather risqué?

CORNELIA: Surely the girls deserve to enjoy themselves! We must keep reminding them, in every action, to discover God present within. Ah, the light-fantastic toe.

(EMILY *plays;* CORNELIA *dances.*)

CORNELIA: And we must find time too for playing some cards... How about whist?

EMILY: Whist, Reverend Mother?

(BISHOP WISEMAN *appears. The dancing and playing abruptly stop.*)

BISHOP W: Mother Connelly, I gather the girls are quite changed, even after a month, as a result of your work at this Convent of the Holy Childhood.

CORNELIA: Here at the Society of the Holy Child Jesus, Bishop, we endeavour to balance activity, instruction, contemplation with a measure of loving care.

BISHOP W: As long as you sow the seeds of piety.

CORNELIA: For this we must also grow new teachers and, most importantly, prune back outstanding debts.

BISHOP W: May you prosper and be blessed in your work.

CORNELIA: Your Grace did promise to find us the funds.

BISHOP W: I can report that I met with Father Connelly.

CORNELIA: Is he well?

BISHOP W: He requested that I advise you to see him again.

CORNELIA: Then let him accept my taking vows.

BISHOP W: I made the matter clear. His objections are withdrawn.

CORNELIA: God be thanked for it.

BISHOP W: There can be no more contact between you.

CORNELIA: Even concerning our children?

BISHOP W: No contact at all.

CORNELIA: This will be wounding for him, I fear.

BISHOP W: Devotion to God, Mother Connelly, is a higher calling than marriage.

CORNELIA: I trust that he understands this better than anyone.

BISHOP W: Be resolute.

(CORNELIA *nods.*)

BISHOP W: Then I may install you as Reverend Mother of this
society. You may also receive the allegiance of its sisters.

CORNELIA: I am ready.

BISHOP W: Yes.

CORNELIA: Yes.

(Bell rings. BISHOP WISEMAN *holds out a Bible.* CORNELIA *steps
forward and places her hand carefully upon the Bible.)*

CORNELIA: Oh, mighty and everlasting God... being most
unworthy of your Divine regard...

I vow poverty.

I vow obedience.

I renew my vow of chastity in the Congregation of the
Holy Child Jesus.

I promise to enter it, to live and to die in it.

(Bishop departs. CORNELIA *withdraws and sits alone in contemplation.* IRIS *opens an instrument case, takes out a flute and assembles it.)*

IRIS: So, flute. Please can we start again?

MAGGIE: From scratch?

IRIS: From scratch.

MAGGIE: OK, a few things to bear in mind.

IRIS: Go on.

MAGGIE: When you take up an instrument you wish you
could play but never learned... or gave up as a child...

IRIS: Because there was no one around to make you practise.

MAGGIE: And also because you might have been impatient,
wanting to play anything straight away, and when it
sounded stilted—

IRIS: Or squeaked—

MAGGIE: You got cross and gave up instead of persevering—

IRIS: Totally frustrating.

MAGGIE: Exactly. So, it can feel like you're at the bottom of a mountain, high, steep and craggy and you're so little, don't know how to climb, might even be afraid of heights—

IRIS: Is this meant to be encouraging?

MAGGIE: What if you approach the instrument as if meeting a new friend for the first time, and you need to get to know each other… little by little… Remember to be friendly towards it, because you want to play together, don't you?

(IRIS *blows into her flute, trying the keys.* PIERCE *appears. He approaches* EMILY.)

PIERCE: May I please see my wife?

EMILY: She is not available.

PIERCE: Tell her that I have withdrawn Adeline from school and taken her to Rome.

EMILY: I will pass on your message.

PIERCE: And I will wait.

(PIERCE *paces. Time ticks.*)

EMILY: Mother Cornelia…?

CORNELIA: What is he doing here?

EMILY: He says that he wants to see you.

CORNELIA: Please inform him that this is not possible.

(PIERCE *paces*.)

EMILY: I am afraid, Mr Connelly—
PIERCE: I will continue to wait.

(PIERCE *paces. Time ticks. A bell chimes.* IRIS *slowly practises a scale.* EMILY *approaches* CORNELIA.)

CORNELIA: Is he still here?

(EMILY *nods*.)

CORNELIA: He promised to do nothing with any of our children without my consent. He must stop returning my letters to them unopened. And he must bring my daughter back to her school.

(EMILY *departs.* CORNELIA *withdraws into herself.* PIERCE *paces. Time ticks. Clock chimes.* EMILY *approaches* PIERCE.)

PIERCE: And would she be so indisposed if some bishop or confessor was in this parlour?
EMILY: It's not my place to say.
PIERCE: Do you also bow without question to those lofty bishops whose instructions she is so ready to obey?
EMILY: Mother Cornelia has her own mind.

(EMILY *does not move*.)

PIERCE: You may stand there in your worn-out boots and widow's weeds for as long as you like. I can outstay all of you.

(EMILY *remains still and silent.* IRIS *plays the scale more quickly; starts to find flow.*)

PIERCE: I will not leave here until I have spoken with her.

EMILY: May I humbly remind you—

PIERCE: Remind me of what... that I've been ostracised for so very long... that you all wish me not to 'interfere' with your precious society? Only let me remind you... and her... that I exist... See. You cannot any of you make me go away and you cannot deny my... my... my... role. For I have a role.

EMILY: No harm is meant, I assure you.

PIERCE: My purpose is expressly... not... It is not to interfere...

EMILY: It would be better for all—

PIERCE: Go and get her, please.

(EMILY *withdraws.*)

PIERCE: I shall stay here... right here.

(PIERCE *lies down and settles in. Elsewhere,* CORNELIA *is alone.* IRIS *attempts a phrase of Chopin's 'Adieu' waltz.*)

PIERCE: It's me, Nelie.

(*Piano picks up the waltz.*)

PIERCE: This priesthood is not the vocation I had hoped. I am ready to return. My arms are open. Let me release you from all these trials of the so-called holy life... Come back, Nelie... We can collect the children... Ady longs to see you. Let us be reconciled to each other... together, a family again... Let's leave this cold, thankless, damp existence behind and sail home. Come, where's your hand? Give me your hand. A man shall leave his father and mother. And hold fast to his wife. And the two shall become... one flesh.

(*Silence.*)

CORNELIA: To do anything well... we must give all our heart, mind, strength, for the love of God.

(*Clock chimes one... two...*)

CORNELIA: Step by step. Act after act. So we must learn. Second by second. Minute after minute...

(*Clock chimes three... four...*)

CORNELIA: Hour after hour after hour after hour after...

(*Clock chimes five and six.*)

PIERCE: Be informed! I shall report to Merty, Ady and Frank that I have been to see their mother. I shall tell them that I waited for an entire six hours. All in vain. To hell with the lot of you!

(PIERCE *abruptly goes.* IRIS *plays another phrase from Chopin's waltz.*)

MAGGIE: You have been practicing.

IRIS: I'm aiming for that thing where the waltz is playing me.

(MAGGIE *laughs*.)

IRIS: I'm going to Dad's next week to get some of my old stuff. Is there anything you'd like – if I can find it?

MAGGIE: Are there any photos of you and Luke growing up?

IRIS: I'll see what there is.

MAGGIE: Will you ask Luke if it's OK?

IRIS: Actually, I better hadn't… not of him… he'd kill me.

MAGGIE: OK.

IRIS: Sorry… I know you hope he might shift, but believe me, you truly don't know what he's like… But still, I'm going to tell Dad that I've been in touch with you for two years…

MAGGIE: That's good.

IRIS: Working out whether to do it after getting the stuff and phone him… Or face to face… If I dare…

(*A bell rings.* CORNELIA *walks to where* PIERCE *had stood*.)

CORNELIA: Is he at last gone? Might it have been wiser to have seen him. Have I caused unnecessary injury or harm? O, Blessed Mother, how am I to be resolute when the temptation is so pressing to heed the struggles of this woman's heart? Ady, Merty and Frank, let me face this test. By devoting myself utterly to my sacred path, so I devote myself to the great Father of us all, and, along with myself, entrust you, dearest children, into His care.

MAGGIE: Are you still frightened of your dad?

IRIS: Not so much now... only when I'm with him sometimes... if things are touchy... Not at a distance... and
Amir helps.

MAGGIE: I'm glad you found Amir.

IRIS: I'm glad you found Mike.

MAGGIE: Really?

IRIS: You deserve him.

MAGGIE: I can't believe you just said that.

IRIS: I mean it.

(*They hug.*)

MAGGIE: Let me know how you get on.

(*A bell rings. The 'Adieu' waltz plays on the piano.*)

CORNELIA: I, Cornelia, vow to have contact in future with
my children, with their father... only when this is con-
sistent with my holy vows for the greater glory of God...
and to pray each day with a full heart for all to be well,
for the higher good of us all.

(CORNELIA *removes her wedding ring from her left hand.*)

16

CONJUGAL RIGHTS

PIERCE *is meeting* MR HARTING, *solicitor.*

HARTING: Injustice, you say?

PIERCE: It is not the injustice towards me that drives me on, but the justice that I owe to others.

HARTING: Most lofty.

PIERCE: I understand that you are an Anglican and a lawyer.

HARTING: I understand that you are a Roman Catholic and a priest.

PIERCE: I am a husband and father first.

HARTING: Is this permitted for a priest?

PIERCE: I shall not be one for very much longer.

HARTING: Very sensible.

PIERCE: And I cannot live as a Roman Catholic either.

HARTING: I understand that your wife is a nun, living in a convent?

PIERCE: For that we can blame those damn bishops.

HARTING: Even though you wanted her to go there in the first place?

PIERCE: I took an oath to protect her.

HARTING: You appear to have taken many oaths, Mr Connelly.

PIERCE: Faith, fidelity, honour I will never forsake, nor will I abandon the mother of my children, despite their attempts to make me. Under their rule, she has been—

HARTING: Corrupted?

PIERCE: Rooted up. Mrs Connelly is in the hands of devils. I must do everything possible to rescue her.

HARTING: Then we shall apply to be granted a decree for Restitution of Conjugal Rights.

PIERCE: Oh, I'm quite content, if necessary, for us to continue as we were... to live as brother and sister...

HARTING: The law, Mr Connelly, admits of no such saintly idea as husband and wife living as siblings. Husband and father, you say?

PIERCE: Until the end.

HARTING: Then declare your desire to cohabit fully. Demand that she be returned to you bed and board.

PIERCE: Very well. Go ahead. Yes.

HARTING: Yes.

(HARTING *leaves.* CORNELIA *appears. Piano plays Verdi's 'Waltz in F Major' in strident reprise.* PIERCE *and* CORNELIA *state/dance their cases, confronting one another.*)

PIERCE: You see before you the first priest for centuries to continue to live with his wife...

CORNELIA: How did we live together? He left me in Grand Coteau. In Rome he visited once a week in the presence of the children and their maid—

PIERCE: She was only required to vow chastity... and now she is imprisoned within convent walls—

CORNELIA: He encouraged me to become a novice—

PIERCE: My consent was subject always to my control—

CORNELIA: He knows that novices are subject only to the control of the Church—

PIERCE: Let her return at once to her home—

CORNELIA: For the good of my soul I pray never to return in any way at all.

PIERCE: I want only to obtain the release of my wife and restore her to her family—

CORNELIA: For 'release of', read 'power over'.

PIERCE: My eyes have now been opened to the false and fatal step I took in entering the Church of Rome—

CORNELIA: No one's eyes were ever truly opened by pride, vanity or disappointed ambition—

PIERCE: For the honour of human nature, let there be full, legitimate, marital reconciliation between us.

(*They dance; music abruptly ends.*)

CORNELIA: Thank God.
PIERCE: No.
CORNELIA: You have your judgement. Let it end here.
PIERCE: This is an outrage.

(CORNELIA *departs.*)

PIERCE: I call upon the House of Commons! (*Raises a handful of pamphlets.*) I oppose this vile Catholic Church with its medieval practices. I challenge the devilish bishops with their insidious creed. I denounce the convents which in truth are no more than prisons. Had I sufficient funds, I would fight on in the highest courts in the land. Failing that, with all my might I must protect my children from every harmful, pernicious influence. Merty, come. And Ady. You too, Frank.

(MERTY, ADY, *in their teens, and* FRANK, *around ten, join their father.*)

ADY: Are we to go away again, Papa?
PIERCE: Children, if I have been remiss... if I have erred... I assure you that I have suffered and daily repent for it...
MERTY: Is this about Mama?
PIERCE: I can do no more. When Rome depraves the heart, the work is not done by half.
ADY: Is she never coming back?
PIERCE: I'm afraid that the fountain of all natural affection has been so dried up within your mother that she has forgotten you.
FRANK: Is it because she's a nun?
PIERCE: And now loves only those so-called holy sisters who have replaced us all.
ADY: May we write to her?
PIERCE: I'm sorry to say that all attempts to reach her have failed. I gather that she's been moved far away to the south coast.
ADY: What if she writes to us?

PIERCE: I assure you that she will not be in contact with any of you.

MERTY: Will we see her again?

PIERCE: She has wilfully abandoned us. We are shut out.

ADY: What will we do?

PIERCE: You'll return to your schools. I have important matters to attend to here in England for the time being. And Merty, if you still wish to return to America when you leave school, you might stay with your uncle in New Orleans. Always remember, we have each other.

MERTY, ADY, FRANK: Yes, Papa.

(*Distorted 'Mary Had a Little Lamb' plays.*)

17

BELL TOLLS

Waves and wind. MIKE *and* MAGGIE *walk along the beach together.*

MAGGIE: Would it help to write to Pete?

MIKE: Is this because of Iris?

MAGGIE: How can I not do anything when it's partly my fault?

MIKE: Has his behaviour ever been your fault?

MAGGIE: It's certainly not hers.

MIKE: What would you say?

MAGGIE: 'Do you really want to lose contact with your daughter? Do you think that by making her choose between us, she'll stop having anything to do with me now? Can't you see that you're making her want to get away from you?'

MIKE: I honestly don't think this is any of your business, love.

MAGGIE: I knew you'd say that.

MIKE: She's not a kid. It's between Iris and her dad now.

(Violinist as MERTY, *now twenty, opens the violin case, takes up violin and bow.)*

MAGGIE: What about contacting Luke?

MIKE: If his dad's cutting off Iris, then it makes it harder for him.

MAGGIE: At least he's still talking to her.

MIKE: You know what I'm going to say.

MAGGIE: It's not up to me to make the approach.

MIKE: If it's going to happen…

MAGGIE: Did I spend more time with Iris when he was little? Did I share more with her? I knew it was too soon.

MIKE: It can only be when he chooses.

MAGGIE: What if he never does?

MIKE: That's very possible.

MAGGIE: You're no bloody comfort.

MIKE: Since when is comfort what you really want?

(MERTY *plays Handel's 'Sonata in E Major' on the violin.* ADY, *now in her late teens, joins* PIERCE.)

ADY: Merty seems to be happy enough in New Orleans, Papa.
  (*She takes a letter out of her sleeve and hands it to her father.*)
  Although our uncle does urge him to take communion.

PIERCE: I hope he has the character to keep his back turned.

ADY: I think so.

PIERCE: Never be tempted or cajoled to return into that Papish mire. It will suck a soul down.

ADY: We are out of it, I promise.

PIERCE: Out of it now for good.

(MERTY *continues to play the sonata. He starts to falter, becoming hot, feverish, unwell, struggles to keep going, loses track. Perhaps odd phrases of 'Mary Had A Little Lamb' randomly interrupt as he keeps trying to pick up, coughs, wipes his brow, has to pause for breath until, exhausted, the music and playing become far too much for him. Silence.* MERTY *lays down the violin in its case. He departs.*)

PIERCE: Merty?

ADY: I'm here, Papa.

PIERCE: Ady, yellow fever can be quick, can't it?

ADY: I truly hope so.

PIERCE: Not hour upon hour of torment. Are you still here, Ady?

ADY: Yes, Papa, I'm still here. Always, Papa.

PIERCE: You promise?

ADY: Yes.

PIERCE: And Frank.

ADY: Would you like me to write and tell him?

PIERCE: We'll go to his school. We shall see him together.

ADY: Need we write to anyone else that poor Merty... Tell anyone else that he is gone?

PIERCE: Who else is there for us to tell?

(*Darkness. Chapel bell tolls once.* CORNELIA *appears. Bell tolls a second and third time.*)

CORNELIA: Is that the chapel bell? Why is it tolling in the middle of the night when no one is pulling the ropes? How can the convent bell ring so, of its own accord?

(MAGGIE *enters the chapel, the child's violin case in her hands.*)

CORNELIA: How did he become ill? Did he suffer? How long was he burning with fever? Did anyone cradle him in their arms? Oh, Mother of Sorrows, do you reveal to me again what you bear? No priest at his bedside? Mercer Connelly, my dear son, I pray for your lost soul.

MAGGIE: 'Dear Luke, I've been keeping your violin here safe for you since the last time I visited. I understand why you did that. I don't blame you at all. I never wanted to leave you when you were little. I couldn't stay with your father. This is not an excuse for the damage caused. It's the truth. You deserve to know it. You are in my heart always, no matter what. You deserve to know this too. It is my deep hope that one day we will meet, find a way to make amends. It is my deepest hope that you're well and thriving. This violin is yours. It's time I returned it to you. With love, Mum.' I pray, Cornelia, for this somehow to get through to him.

(MAGGIE *places the violin case beside* CORNELIA.)

18

ST LEONARDS

CORNELIA *plays the piano, reminding herself of Chopin's 'Adieu' waltz. After a moment, she takes up her notebook and writes.*

CORNELIA: Each teacher must strive at all times to instil in the hearts of their pupils the love and virtues of the Holy Child Jesus by practicing humility and gentleness…

(ADY, *now in her late twenties, approaches. She coughs politely.*)

CORNELIA: Ady?

ADY: Please don't let me interrupt you.

CORNELIA: How was your journey?

ADY: The train was comfortable, thank you.

CORNELIA: I'm so pleased you're able to visit at last.

ADY: It seemed remiss not to, since we've been staying over the weekend in Brighton and our hosts were most encouraging about your school. So we felt it worth seeing when the opportunity arose.

CORNELIA: I hope you found us easily.

ADY: St Leonards not being so very big, it was little trouble to make my way here from the station.

CORNELIA: Did you see some of our girls taking a morning dip?

ADY: In the sea?

CORNELIA: Where else?

ADY: In public?

CORNELIA: The benefits, I advise the bishops, are far more than simply physical, and so swim they shall, whether it is approved of or no. What do you have in your pocket?

(ADY *pulls out a couple of choice pebbles.*)

ADY: Forgive me. I am aware that if everyone took pieces of the beach then there would be none left for anyone else.

CORNELIA: Do you still collect oddments for your scrapbook?

ADY: Occasionally, perhaps.

CORNELIA: What about your sketching and painting?

ADY: I prefer to read more often now. And sew.

CORNELIA: Sewing, really? I'm glad to hear this. And what of your singing and piano playing?

ADY: It's best not to disturb Papa with too much practicing, so I make sure to do it after breakfast when he takes his stroll.

CORNELIA: So, you are well settled.

ADY: Yes, we are both at home in Florence.

CORNELIA: Such a well-endowed and magnificent city. So much art. So many beautiful churches.

ADY: We attend St James's mostly.

CORNELIA: I do not know it.

ADY: The congregation is American, which Papa prefers.

CORNELIA: I still feel that he can never in his heart cease to love the Holy Catholic Church, although his love, I recall, was always more a love of sentiment than of sacrifice. But I hope you might return to the faith.

ADY: The Episcopalian faith suits us both well, thank you.

CORNELIA: Do you hear from Frank?

ADY: His tutor in Paris—

CORNELIA: Is he in Paris now?

ADY: Yes, and his tutor has persuaded him to be fully a sculptor.

CORNELIA: How marvellous.

ADY: Do you approve?

CORNELIA: Sculpture, like painting, is very much a Christian art, is it not?

ADY: I dare say.

CORNELIA: And is he well?

ADY: He is.

CORNELIA: Would you like me to show you around?

ADY: Please do not go to any trouble.

CORNELIA: We have fifteen acres. The cloister is very pretty, the church newly built. The choir are to be rehearsing soon. (*Plays a couple of chords on piano with her left hand.*) Come now, Ady, what about a duet?

ADY: Is this allowed?

CORNELIA: You sound like the bishops.

ADY: I certainly do not intend to. (*Remains rooted to the spot.*) Are any other convent schools like this?

CORNELIA: Stiffness and rigour will not bring forth love, and are not the spirit of the Holy Child. No child, no novice, no sister or mother is quite the same. She must be fully her best self as God would wish her to be. If only you could have spent your school days here.

ADY: Papa and I are quite content with my accomplishments.

CORNELIA: And after looking around would you care for some lunch?

ADY: I would appreciate it. Thank you.

CORNELIA: You're most welcome to stay tonight. Tomorrow we're making an excursion. Would you like to join us?

ADY: I am expected to return to Brighton this evening for dinner with some acquaintances of Papa.

CORNELIA: Then we must make the most of the time we have.

ADY: Where are you going tomorrow?

CORNELIA: We'll climb aboard some carts and be whisked off… well, most likely trundled… to an old palace that is all but ruins, I gather, and our plan is to picnic there.

ADY: Is it far?

CORNELIA: A number of miles. Some singing will pass the ride.

ADY: I wish you a pleasant trip.

CORNELIA: Maybe you'll come again, and we can go together to Mayfield.

ADY: I'm afraid that is unlikely.

(CORNELIA *gets a leather-bound book and hands it to* ADY.)

CORNELIA: This is for you.

ADY: Such fine paper.

CORNELIA: Quality of materials inspires quality of craft.

ADY (*reading inscription*): 'Confidence begets confidence. Persistence wins the crown.' This is too generous.

CORNELIA: It is too little.

ADY: Thank you… Mother.

(ADY *goes.* CORNELIA *watches her, a pall of sadness crossing her face.*)

CORNELIA: Far too little.

(CORNELIA *plays a phrase of Chopin's 'Adieu' waltz.*)

CORNELIA: For a teacher and holy mother is at all times to serve with a love that is noble, tender and disinterested, trusting each one in her care to learn for herself.

(CORNELIA *stops playing and returns to her notebook. Sounds of waves on a beach and seagulls.* MAGGIE *and* IRIS *are balancing rocks upon one another to make a pile.*)

IRIS: And I looked out for Luke. He used to get into fights a lot at school, and with kids in the neighbourhood, and I'd deal with it somehow without Dad finding out, terrified that he would!

MAGGIE: I know, love—

IRIS: No... You don't know... You weren't there...

MAGGIE: You've told me...

IRIS: And all the times Dad lost it or I found him low, saying he didn't know if he could keep going... And how I tried to comfort him. And taking it so seriously when he asked if he could trust us. 'Or are you going to betray me too?' I didn't have the option of giving up or bailing out, did I? And so I didn't argue with him about going to the secondary school where none of my friends were going. And I'd do my homework after making dinner or doing the laundry. And I did the subjects that he wanted and pretended to do the law degree... And I learned to keep my life to myself... And why the hell do I still feel so bloody guilty and disloyal?

MAGGIE: It's not you...

IRIS: And after all I did... to try to help... how come he still can't even bring himself to reply to my birthday invitation? He's had long enough to get used to the appalling idea that I know and love and get on with my mother... Why did I even invite him again after last year and the year before... Why do I keep getting it so wrong?

MAGGIE: It's his loss, honey...

IRIS: At least it's less stress if I really never ever see him again until his funeral... Unless I go first.

MAGGIE: Is that what you really want?

IRIS: I just want to remember next year to leave him off the list.

MAGGIE: You know... when I'm with you... sometimes... I get flashes of seeing him in you... and I feel, 'Thanks, Pete'... because... without him... you wouldn't be who you are.

IRIS: I can't imagine he'd ever see it that way about you.

MAGGIE: He's not the bad guy, any more than I am.

IRIS: Don't let him off the hook. He's kept up this shitty act for most of our lives, and he's still going strong.

MAGGIE: You don't need to carry that either.

IRIS: Some things can't be mended, Mum.

MAGGIE: We're managing OK, you and me, aren't we?

IRIS: That's because we want to.

MAGGIE: And your dad and Luke don't?

IRIS: And never will.

19

WALTZ

THEODORA *plays the opening of 'Bells'.* MAGGIE *approaches.*

MAGGIE: Back at the old chapel piano, Sister Theodora?

THEODORA: I hope I do your piece justice.

MAGGIE: How was your rehearsal with the girls?

THEODORA: I'm glad we have another before the concert.

MAGGIE: Might I say a few words before the performance?

THEODORA: About how you composed 'Bells'?

MAGGIE: And dedicating it, my gift to Cornelia, for all she
    lost, all she made and gave, returning to her what she
    inspires, with your help, sister, something from my best
    self for a very human saint.

THEODORA: I have a feeling that would be appreciated,
    Maggie.

('Bells' continues on piano. MIKE *appears and holds out his hand to*
MAGGIE.)

MAGGIE: Oh, Mike.

MIKE: Well, will you join me?

MAGGIE: But you'll be working...

MIKE: I can add a couple of days... Make it a long weekend...

MAGGIE: I'll have to rejig my schedule...

MIKE: Is that a yes?

MAGGIE: How can I not say yes to Rome?

(*Verdi's 'Waltz in F Major' plays.* MAGGIE *takes* MIKE's *hand. They waltz. Blue sky.*)

MAGGIE: *Esquilino… Palatino… Quirinale… Viminale…*

MIKE: Which is the seventh hill again?

MAGGIE: Aren't we standing on it?

MIKE/MAGGIE: *Aventino.*

(*Flapping of bird wing.*)

MAGGIE: There's someone I want to look up.

MIKE: Oh?

MAGGIE: Come.

(*Rome's Cimitero Acattolico, the non-Catholic cemetery. Graves of Shelley and Keats. Row upon row of tombstones.* MAGGIE *consults the* CORNELIA *book.*)

MIKE: So… if this is *Zona Seconda…*

MAGGIE: Isn't the American section that way?

MIKE: Or is this *Zona Terza…*?

MAGGIE: It doesn't give any detail… Only that he's here somewhere…

(*The grave of 'PIERCE FRANCIS CONNELLY. SCULPTOR.' appears.*)

MIKE: Hey!

MAGGIE: You've found him?

MIKE (*reading*): 'In everlasting memory of the artist... whose life was devoted to creating works of beauty. 1841–1932.'

MAGGIE: 'Pierce Francis Connelly.'

MIKE: 'Sculptor.'

MAGGIE: Frank.

MIKE: 'Son of the late Rev. Pierce Connelly of Philadelphia...'

MAGGIE: 'And Cornelia Peacock Connelly... Foundress of the Society of the Holy Child Jesus...' Well.

MIKE: Surprised?

MAGGIE: He had nothing to do with his mother for most of his life... hated her order and the nuns.

MIKE: 'Dedicated by his loving daughter, Marina Borghese.'

MAGGIE: Frank's love child seems to have brought her grandparents back together.

MIKE: To abide in peace?

(*Flapping of bird wing.* MIKE *sighs and steps forward.*)

MAGGIE: Time for your meeting already?

MIKE: Don't miss me too much.

MAGGIE: Oh, I think I'll make do with a few statues, churches, fountains... Per coin, is it one wish or three?

(*They kiss.*)

MIKE: Have as many damn wishes as you like.

(MIKE *goes. Busy traffic, horns hooting.* MAGGIE *wanders, looking at the book. 'Bells' on piano begins to build.*)

MAGGIE: Palazzo Doria Pamphilj?

(*A chandelier. Dim, luminous light. The golden ballroom.* CORNELIA *and* PIERCE *appear.* PIERCE *swoops up* CORNELIA *and they dance in each other's arms.*)

MAGGIE: Ah, the light-fantastic toe.

(PIERCE *and* CORNELIA *swirl around* MAGGIE... *then disappear. Silence.* YOUNG MAN *enters, with camera, and looks around, scanning the room.*)

YOUNG MAN (*in an English accent*): Scusi...? Em... Posso... *fare delle foto?*
MAGGIE: Sure, feel free.
YOUNG MAN: Oh... right... thanks.
MAGGIE: Bit dim with the shutters closed.
YOUNG MAN: Good to get somewhere not so well known.
MAGGIE: *Uno tesoro nascosto di Roma.*
YOUNG MAN: How's that?
MAGGIE: Hidden treasure of Rome.
YOUNG MAN: OK.

(*He points the camera at different parts of the room.*)

MAGGIE: D'you mind me asking... Is this for work or pleasure?
YOUNG MAN: An assignment... for a course.

(*Silence. The* YOUNG MAN *takes some photos.*)

YOUNG MAN: D'you happen to know what room this is exactly?

MAGGIE: Ballroom.

YOUNG MAN: Thanks.

(MAGGIE *looks at him intently as he continues searching for shots in the dimness.*)

YOUNG MAN: Am I in your way?

MAGGIE: No, it's—

YOUNG MAN: Won't be long…

MAGGIE: Only…

YOUNG MAN: Nearly done…

MAGGIE: It's just that…

YOUNG MAN: None of these will probably come out…

MAGGIE: Are you…?

YOUNG MAN: Maybe a few might… Only need one or two…

MAGGIE: Are you…?

YOUNG MAN: Excuse me?

MAGGIE: Does your name happen to be Luke?

YOUNG MAN: Sorry?

MAGGIE: I'm just wondering…

YOUNG MAN: How do you know?

MAGGIE: So, it is Luke?

LUKE: Yes.

MAGGIE: It's you, isn't it?

LUKE: I don't understand.

MAGGIE: I'm Maggie.

LUKE: Who?

MAGGIE: Remember…?

LUKE: What?

MAGGIE: Recognise me at all?

LUKE: Mum?

MAGGIE: Yes.

LUKE: Jesus.

(*Silence.*)

LUKE: Is this Iris... Did she... Does she tell you where I go?

MAGGIE: I had no idea you were in Rome... or studying photography... That's great...

LUKE: It's nothing to do with you.

MAGGIE: I wouldn't track you down... I'd never—

LUKE: What are you doing here?

MAGGIE: Weekend trip... last minute...

(*Their eyes meet.*)

MAGGIE: What are the chances?

LUKE: You just came in here... for no reason?

MAGGIE: Maybe it's a miracle.

LUKE: What are you talking about?

MAGGIE: Would you like to get a coffee...?

LUKE: I can't.

MAGGIE: Only for a—

LUKE: No... no.

MAGGIE: Are you in Rome for long?

LUKE: I'd better go now.

MAGGIE: OK.

LUKE: Right.

MAGGIE: Take care.

(LUKE *leaves.* MAGGIE *reels slightly and tries to take in what has happened.*)

MAGGIE: Bloody hell.... My God... How did he...?

(*'Bells' starts to build and swell on piano.*)

MAGGIE: How did he come to make his way here...? How at this very same moment... both of us...? How did he make his way here... like me... now...? Did I say the right thing...? Did I say the wrong thing? What else could I have said... or done...? How on earth did he get to be so tall?

(*Violin joins with melody for 'Bells'.* CORNELIA *appears. In this remarkable moment, it becomes clear that the actual ballroom of the Doria Pamphilj and the golden eternal ballroom are one and the same.*)

MAGGIE: That was Luke. He was here. Actually here. Wasn't he?

(CORNELIA *looks directly at* MAGGIE.)

MAGGIE: He spoke to me. Didn't he?

(MAGGIE *looks directly at* CORNELIA.)

MAGGIE: We've spoken now. Haven't we?

(*Their eyes meet.*)

MAGGIE: Yes?

(CORNELIA *moves slightly to the music.*)

MAGGIE: Yes.

(MAGGIE *starts to move to the music.*)

MAGGIE: Yes!

(MAGGIE *and* CORNELIA *dance a messy, joyful, laughing, crying, waltz, all over the place, in the golden ballroom.*)

END

AUTHOR'S NOTE

When I 'bumped into' Ghislaine Kenyon in a cinema foyer towards the end of 2012, I had no idea where this chance encounter would lead. Raised in a Jewish home and community in the north-west of the UK, I knew barely anything about Catholicism, and nothing at all about Cornelia Connelly. From the moment Ghislaine told me about Cornelia's life and educational work, I was compelled to take the adventure that *Waltz With Me* has become. This has included travelling in Cornelia's footsteps and attending an Ash Wednesday service in Mayfield Chapel, where my forehead was dabbed with ash at the beginning of Lent. Then experiencing the Nativity story brought to life, following students transformed into Mary, Joseph, amenable donkey, shepherds and angels up the main street of the town of Mayfield and into the chapel, where a live baby representing the newly born Jesus cried until falling asleep. I have learned more about the power of religious ritual to inform the making of art, beyond the confines of dogma and belief, particularly in theatre, and, like Cornelia and Maggie, rediscovered afresh, through combining their stories, how important are singing, music and dance to help bear the most painful experiences and live the fullest, most beautiful life possible.

There follow a few nuggets I encountered along the way.

One of the key sources informing the writing of *Waltz With Me* was *Positio: Documentary Study for the Canonisation Process of the Servant of God, Cornelia Connelly, Née Peacock (1809–1879)*.

This comprehensive compilation in three volumes of all documentation of Cornelia's life, family, work was typed up over many years by nuns in SHCJ, the order that she founded. It is currently in the hands of the Vatican, pending approval.

I wonder if *Waltz With Me* is one of the very few – or perhaps only – plays to be sourced, in part, from an application for sainthood.

'When Bishop Grant was told that the children at St Leonards "waltzed, danced the polka and played whist", he ordered the dancing to stop.'

Sister Anne Murphy, SOURCE: Studies and Reflections on the Heritage of the Society of the Holy Child Jesus, Summer 1988

'Cornelia Connelly is so much more than an historical figure of the past. Her spirit remains accessible and responsive today to anyone who asks. I am living proof. I was introduced to Cornelia as a thirteen-year-old student at a Holy Child high school in the USA. One of the sisters gave me a copy of a biography about her that I promptly put on a shelf and forgot. Thirty years later, as I sadly concluded my marriage was so harmful that I would have to seek divorce, I was dusting off a shelf where I came across the book, paging through it for the first time. Suddenly, Cornelia's story had a whole new resonance as I voraciously read it cover to cover. When

I finally put it down, I promptly had a conversation with her, telling her that I understood she had no power to protect her children after separation from her husband because she had no rights to do so. I told her that times have changed, and although I had rights now that she didn't have, I was still asking for her help with my daughters, whose well-being was my highest priority. I asked her fervently to help me protect them from any adverse consequences from an impending, frightening and contentious divorce. Together we would work to ensure that my children had a better, more secure outcome than hers did. It would be an opportunity for her to have a "do over" while I promised to do everything I could to share her story with others. I had a distinct sensation that she agreed, and a pact was made. I am happy and relieved to say that today my children are stable, kind, loving and productive adults and mothers. I know that the hope and support Cornelia gave me was responsible for this outcome, and I have kept my promise to share her story whenever possible. Our friendship continues to this day...'

> *Letter from an audience member after attending presentation*
> *of work in progress, Philadelphia, 2017*

Cornelia Connelly's Tomb at Mayfield Chapel

A sketch of Cornelia while a novice at Sacred Heart in Rome

Cornelia as a younger woman at the time of her marriage

Cornelia as Reverend Mother, Superior General of the SHCJ

Mayfield 1863–1893 – south-east view

St Leonards – courtyard with pupils, late 1880s

Pierce Connelly

Frank Connelly aged 18 and Adeline Connelly aged 23

Angel on Frank Connelly's grave

ACKNOWLEDGEMENTS

Many, many thanks to all who have given their time, energy, shared their experience, insights, expertise and resourced the remarkable adventure of discovery and synchronicity that researching and writing this play has turned out to be.

Ghislaine Kenyon for telling me Cornelia's story in the first place, research, consultancy, and for support in uncountable ways throughout, worthy winner of the Writers' Guild of Great Britain's Olwen Wymark Theatre Encouragement Award, 2017.

Titania Krimpas and Deborah Vogt for dramaturgy.

David Osmond for original compositions, including 'Bells', piano playing, acting, musical direction. Laura Forrest Hay for music consultation. Richard Peirson and Simona Budd for tracking down musical scores, accompanying on piano during development workshops.

Joe Harmston for producing, directing, casting, support and guidance.

Marcel and Sophia Kral at Smallfish Designs for flyers and cover image.

Sister Judith Lancaster for invaluable information, sharing her experience and insights, making connections.

Christina Latham-Koenig for invaluable support and encouragement.

Gaye Donaldson, family constellations therapist, for enabling us to probe the depths of the individual character and family dynamics.

Isabel Keating and Helen Forshaw, curators of Cornelia Connelly archive for access to original documents, artefacts, photos.

Monica Matthews and the Society of the Holy Child Jesus for funding the research process and continuing support and encouragement.

All at Casa Cornelia, Rome, Italy, including Carmen Torres, for hospitality, open-hearted sharing of their lives and work.

Nuns interviewed: Marguerite Bouteloup; Doreen Casey; Eileen Crowley; Mary Lalor; Anne Murphy.

In the USA, Philadelphia and New York: Mary Ann Buckley; Sam Strike; Peg Doyle; Helen McDonald; pianist Nicole Baker; Matt Ronzani; Lea Murtaugh; Lynn Rothenhoefer; Rochelle Gauger; Christyn Moran; Jake Ferry; Anita Martineau; Dr Sharon Hirsch; Joan Cavanagh; Claire Cumberland; Michael Staton; Kim Calhoun; Toni Archibald; Melissa Dan; Heather Raftery; Josh Luxenbourg; Caroline Erisman.

In Santiago, Chile: Alicia Rojas; Marta Carrión; Ascensión Moreno; Elizabeth Stroub.

All at Mayfield School including head-teacher Antonia Beary, especially, for support with workshops, first reading of the earliest draft, Helen Halliday, Claire Ball, Katie Chamberlain, Karen Bowles; Natasha Evans; Sally.

Professional support: Caroline Underwood; David Micklem; Neil Marcus.

Those supporting research, workshops and readings: Rachel Kraftman; Barbara Susman; Amy Dowding; May Cornet; Marianne Powell; Jake Garfield; Tamara Micner; Carole Pluckrose; Sakuntala Ramanee; Caroline Sax; Deborah Ward; Hazel Gould; Alex Bowen; Kathleen O'Hara; Eleanor Sullivan; Tori Clay; Izzy Goatcher; Summer Balfour; Amelia Gabriel; Georgie Weston; Kitty Evans-Smith; Darcie Genier; Amanda McHugh; Darren Munn, Noemi Gunea; Bo Ashby-Crane; Father Dominic Jacob; Katey Fraser; Claire Price; Jennie Stoller; Ken Christiansen; Jessica Martin; Sarah Gabriel; Hannah Bristow; Leonie Hill; Niamh Cusack; Finbar Lynch; Eric Sirakian; Ellie Burrow; Ria Butler; Ben Hall; Danny Sapani; Lydia Leonard; Polly Meynell; Hannah Blaikie; Louis Landau; Imogen Slaughter; Lizzy Watts; Alice Barron: Matilda Rowe; Lucy Cullingford; Patrick Dineen; Sarah Mowat.

All at JW3, London for providing workshop space, resources, support, mounting presentations, particularly Mekella Broomberg, Greg Blank and Graham Self.

Will Dady at Renard Press for publishing the play and Miriam Halahmy for introducing us to one another.

And thanks for always being there to my partner Paul Berrill.